T0078310

ALSO BY MICHAEL WALSH

Who's Afraid of Classical Music?

Andrew Lloyd Webber: His Life and Works

Carnegie Hall: The First One Hundred Years

A Highly
Opinionated,
Informative,
and Entertaining
Guide to
Appreciating
Opera

Michael Walsh

A FIRESIDE BOOK *Published by Simon & Schuster*

Who's Afraid of Opera?

New York London Toronto Sydney Tokyo Singapore

FIRESIDE
Rockefeller Center
1230 Avenue of the Americas
New York, New York 10020

Designed by Pei Loi Koay

Manufactured in the United States of America

3 4 5 6 7 8 9 10

Library of Congress Cataloging-in-Publication Data
Walsh, Michael (Michael Allen)
Who's afraid of opera? : a highly opinionated, informative,
and entertaining guide to appreciating opera /
Michael Walsh.
p. cm.
"A Fireside book." Includes index.
1. Operas—Analysis, appreciation. I. Title.
MT95.W28 1994
782. 1—dc20 94-29619 CIP

ISBN 0-671-88402-6

For Clare Veronica Walsh, a natural performer

Contents

Introduction, or Why Opera?

Thanks to you, this book is a sequel. In 1988, in response to an almost weekly barrage of queries about how to "get into" classical music from friends, acquaintances, and readers of my musical criticism in *Time* magazine, I wrote *Who's Afraid of Classical Music?* (I wanted to call it *Who's Afraid of Hugo Wolf?*, but the reference was felt to be too obscure.) At that time, there were a number of perfectly adequate introductions to concert music on the market, but each of them seemed to me to be aimed at the reader who was already interested in, and to a certain extent familiar with, the norms of classical music—the etiquette, lore, and terminology those of us in the business take for granted, but which may strike outsiders as mysterious, pretentious, arrogant, and daunting, not necessarily in that order.

So the thought occurred to me: why not write a book that presupposed *absolutely no knowledge of music* on the part of the reader? For the sake of my sanity, I had to assume that anyone picking up the book would at least be vaguely curious about classical music, but otherwise I posited zero knowledge of the field. My hypothetical reader came armed with his or her intellectual curiosity—call me old-fashioned, but I believe such things still exist in Beavis and Butt-head America, if only in isolated pockets of resistance—and a willingness to indulge my frequent nonmusical images and a deliberately breezy tone that was nearly guaranteed to alienate my fellow professionals.

Write the book I did, and I haven't regretted it for a minute. I treasure all the letters from those readers who found it helpful, valuable, and even amusing, and I am pleased that a number of American orchestras are using it as a painless introduction to the mysteries of the classical organism for their younger and newer subscribers. The book even caught the eye of the producers of NBC's *Today Show,* on which I appeared bright and early one morning to sit, somewhat ridiculously, at a white grand piano and demonstrate to Deborah Norville the melodic similarities between Andrew Lloyd Webber's "I Don't Know How to Love Him" from *Jesus Christ Superstar* and the lyrical second theme from the Funeral March movement of Chopin's Second Piano Sonata.

And you bought the book—enough of you, anyway, to have kept it in print since publication and for it to have gone into second and third editions. Although that volume treated opera in some detail, there was obviously not enough space to adequately discuss what is, after all, a way of life in its own right. This book, therefore, became inevitable at a certain point.

However, it had to wait awhile. In 1989 I left the United States to live in Europe and write about foreign affairs. With impeccable timing, I got there the same year the Berlin Wall came crashing down, the Eastern Bloc collapsed under its own dead weight, and, finally, the Soviet Union itself disappeared into the ash can of history. For most of this period I wrote little about classical music; having been a professional music critic since 1973, I needed a break from an art I loved too much to continue to watch slide into artistic irrelevance. It was far more interesting, rewarding, and considerably less frustrating, to hang out with the *mafiozniki* in Moscow, to chat with the leader of the only functioning Jewish congregation in Warsaw, to tour the fine breweries of Bohemia and to sip the exquisite nectar of Pilsener Urquell and Czech Budweiser ("the beer of kings") straight from the source. In short, to watch a world die, change, and be painfully, but optimistically, reborn.

About the chances of survival of classical music, I was considerably less sanguine. Much of the snobbish image of our field we can blame directly on ourselves, on the cult of personality that has, Stalin-like, afflicted music since even before the war. In a kind of reverse, perverse Marxism-Leninism, we embraced the indefensible premise that musical history had ended sometime around 1935, that all the good music that would ever be written already had been written, and that the function of performers from here to eternity would henceforth be to worship at the shrine of the Great Composers, to endlessly regurgitate the Great Masterworks for the edification of a dwindling corps of true believers.

This is the not the place to go into the historical reasons for such developments. Suffice it to say that six years later I am more hopeful about the state of classical music than I was during the go-go eighties. The defeat of that most pernicious form of musical Stalinism, the twelve-tone system, by a group of courageous composers signaled the end of the belief that music history had ended. Just as in Russia, there would be no paradigmatic New Soviet Man in music; the Schoenberg revolution fell as hard as the statue of Felix Dzerzhinsky when it came crashing down in front of KGB headquarters in Moscow. And if we no longer have the commandments to guide us, we are better off in our freedom, however messy and anarchic it may prove to be.

What has all this got to with opera? you ask. Plenty. If music and opera are dead art forms, then there would be no need for this book. If the repertoire closed some sixty years ago, then you could just pick up Deems Taylor and be done with it. But opera has proved itself more resilient than the conformists imagined; despite their protestations, it has flourished over the past half decade. A thousand flowers have bloomed: not only Philip Glass's minimalism but John Adams's variety; not only John Corigliano's flamboyant conservatism but Bill Bolcom's.

Young composers across the country have turned to opera and musical theater with a vengeance (in John Moran's *The Manson Family,* sometimes literally), finding in it the most liberating venue for their imaginations and renewing the form in precisely the way it should and must be invigorated if our musical culture is to stagger into the twenty-first century.

In the meantime, American opera companies have suddenly shown themselves to be far more hospitable to new works and new productions of old works than they were in even the recent past. In Chicago, Lyric Opera director Ardis Krainik has embarked on an ambitious program of new American operas—and this in the house that used to be called, not always flatteringly, La Scala West. Even the staid Metropolitan Opera in New York, the country's Mother Church of European operatic culture, surprised everybody during the 1992–93 season with the premieres of Glass's *The Voyage* and Corigliano's *The Ghosts of Versailles.* New opera is suddenly hot, big box office, a development that can only bring joy to those of us who would like to see content-free singing contests such as Francesco Cilèa's *Adriana Lecouvreur* slip from the repertoire in favor of something with, shall we say, a little more substance.

So let me state my point of view clearly, right up front. If you are a vocal nut, if you only attend opera to cheer your favorite diva, if you rush down the aisle and hurl a bouquet of flowers the size of the Manhattan phone book at the object of your affection, then this book is not for you. Although many contemporary singers will be mentioned in these pages, this is not a discussion of whether Pavarotti is better than Domingo, or vice versa; nor will it take a stand on the burning question of whether Callas was a greater diva than Renata Tebaldi. Although I will recommend some recordings in the Discography, it is not a guide to the best performances on disk, for nothing ages faster than a list that is out of date even before it is published. If you're looking for this sort of thing, then you will have to look elsewhere.

What I offer in its stead is a philosophy of listening to and understanding opera. There is an old saying that if you give a starving man a fish, you have fed him; if you teach him how to fish, on the other hand, he can feed himself. It would be easy to give you a series of opera recommendations—repertoire, performers, venues, recordings—and send you off into the world, waving this book the way the budget tourists in France used to wave Arthur Frommer's *Europe on $5 a Day* back in the sixties. But, as former president Nixon (whose destruction of the Bretton Woods agreement did so much to ensure those days of strong dollars would never come again) might say: it would be wrong.

In the end, the best way for you to come to opera is on your own. Your taste is your own; and while you and I may share a fondness for certain composers or works, our tastes will never match exactly. The first opera I ever got to know was, of all things, Alban Berg's *Wozzeck*, widely regarded as one of the thorniest and most difficult scores of the twentieth century (it's not, but that's another story). I wouldn't necessarily recommend starting out with Berg, but because nobody told me it was supposed to be so tough I got to know it intimately; it held no terrors for me, and to this day, I regard it as one of the century's most beautiful, moving scores. You may want to start out with something "simpler": Puccini's *La bohème* perhaps, or Verdi's *Il trovatore;* that's up to you.

What I'm trying to do in the pages that follow is to expose you to the marvelous variety of opera, and guide you to certain works I find especially rewarding or noteworthy. But even more important, I'm trying to help you to develop your own *philosophy of opera.* If you read the first book, you know that I overwhelmingly favor the music over the performer and if I succeed in one thing, I hope it is that you should too.

So you'll learn what opera is, and isn't, and how to listen to it. You'll get an overview of operatic history, how and why the art form developed the way it did. We'll discuss that age-old question: which is more important, the words or the music, and come up with an answer. There is a long central chapter in which a basic repertoire is proposed; after that, among other things, we'll examine nonoperatic operas, the physiology and psychology of singing, and what we're going to do once (gulp) we're actually in the theater.

So curtain up! It's time to settle into our seats—two on the aisle, if you please—tuck the programs under our seats, fold our hands on our laps and watch the house lights go down. And get ready for the musical ride of our lives.

Chapter 1

What Opera Is—and What It's Not, or How I Got Here

The opera is like a husband with a foreign title: expensive to support, hard to understand, and therefore a supreme social challenge.

—CLEVELAND AMORY

Opera is like an oyster; it must be swallowed whole, or not at all.

—SPIKE HUGHES AND BARBARA MCFADYEAN, *NIGHTS AT THE OPERA*

Acting is very, very important in opera. But, of course, it is just as well if you also have a voice.

—OPERA SINGER TITO GOBBI

Let's start with what opera is not. It's easier that way.

Opera is not, as Dr. Samuel Johnson famously, if perhaps apocryphally, noted, an "exotic and irrational entertainment." Nor is it, in the immortal wisecrack of Mark Twain, "as bad as it sounds." (He was speaking of Wagner, but he could have been thinking about anybody.)

It's not boring. It's not just for rich people, or society people, or gay people. It's not just for the middle-aged or the middlebrow. It's not just something you trek up to the Metropolitan Opera or the San Francisco Opera or the Lyric of Chicago or any of the many other fine American opera houses to see, witness with awe, and then head home again to forget all about it.

Even though you thought it might be all of the above, in fact it's none of those things. What opera is, beyond dispute, is:

- the greatest art form yet invented by humankind
- the most beautiful music ever written for the voice
- the grandest stage spectacle extant

Imagine a combination of golden song, magnificent symphonic music, riveting theater, and brilliant dance, and you will come up with . . . opera. From the beginning, opera was meant to be a glorious synthesis of all the arts, and over the course of centuries, it has developed into all that and more. I don't think it's too much to say that opera is the monarch of all the arts, the highest and noblest artistic endeavor.

If that sounds a little extravagant, as if I'm overstating the case, let's consider the facts. From its birth in late-sixteenth-century Italy, opera was intended to be the art form to end all art forms, to combine the best features of each of the performing arts into one seamless, exciting whole. Opera combines the drama of the theater with the emotional power of music and the grace and beauty of dance. Until it came along, you had to buy each element separately; once it was up and running, one-stop shopping was evermore the rule.

A common criticism leveled against opera is that it's not realistic, that we don't conduct our lives in song, that people normally don't go around giving voice to their innermost thoughts (in opera, these are almost always about sex) or singing for ten minutes despite just having received a fatal stab wound or gunshot, or falling down dead of a broken heart just as the curtain is coming down.

Well, excuuuuuuse me! Of course opera's artificial and stylized: that's just the point. Since when is that a crime? As Goethe noted in a letter to Schiller (amazing, when you think about it, that the two greatest German dramatists were living and working in the same small city, Weimar): "Opera is free from any servile imitation of nature. By the power of music it attunes the soul to a beautiful receptiveness." The fault lies not in opera but in ourselves.

Conditioned by the movies, television, and an increasingly stupid popular culture to prize and expect "realism"—indeed, to confuse realism with art—American audiences have been losing the capacity to separate art from artifice for the past three decades or so. The triumph of the moving image over the written word, which is really the triumph of brute empiricism over the imagination, has resulted in a culture that cannot distinguish between reality and fantasy.

And so we get, often within months of their real-life manifestations, quickie made-for-TV movies about the crime or scandale du jour: Amy and Joey (surely last names are not necessary here); homicidal Texas cheerleader moms; and stranglers, murderers, and rapists of every description. One can practically sense criminals lining up, a blackjack or a bomb in one hand and their agent's beeper number in the other; the real way crime pays today is in selling the book, television, and movie rights. Not only lawyers chase ambulances these days; producers are right behind them.

A hundred, even fifty years ago, few were disturbed by opera's flagrant inattention to "realistic" detail because they knew there was more to opera than simply watching human beings on stage. On the contrary, opera is rich in realism, and in a way that predates Freud. *Opera's reality is not that of the streets, the byways, and the gutters, but that of the emotions and the mind.* Once we have that straight, all else follows.

If this book can teach you one thing, it is that opera is not about extravagant plots and elaborate sets, although it certainly has these. It is not about cult of personality that has always surrounded the art form's biggest (in more ways than one) stars, from Patti to Pavarotti. It's not about having a box at the Met—although the Met was founded because a group of Manhattan society swells were stuck in the cheap seats at the old Academy of Music—or wearing a monkey suit or a new evening gown on opening night. It's not even about singing, although singing is certainly one of its most important components.

It's about music and how, through music, we examine our common humanity.

Amazingly, many people miss this salient aspect of the operatic experience. They go for any or all of the reasons listed above, but they miss the deeper—and more important—level upon which opera exercises its hold on our imaginations. Sure, it's fun to yell "Bravo!" or "Brava!" at the latest vocal wonder, to tear up your program into little strips and rain down homemade confetti on the heads of those sitting in the orchestra seats, or stalls (as the British call them, as if the folks there were horses), or the parquet, as the main floor of theaters in Paris is called (and the basketball court at the Boston Garden). Sure it's fun to debate the relative merits of conductor, stage director (increasingly important today in what Huizinga or Spengler might have called the late-crystallization phase of our musical culture), set designer, and cast after the show is over.

None of this, however, is what opera is all about. Instead, opera is about the exploration of the heart and soul, about how our deepest desires and longings influence and affect our behavior and touch the lives of the people around us. Through the medium of music, opera reaches us on a level that theater, which is bound to the spoken word and the representative action, can only dream about. In opera, there are always two levels of meaning going on simultaneously, and don't think the best composers aren't aware of it. Take this example:

In the great Letter Scene from Act I of Tchaikovsky's *Eugene Onegin* [say oh-NYAY-gin], which is based on the poem by Pushkin, the most beloved of Russian poets, Tatiana pours out her emotions in an extraordinary epistle addressed to the man, the cold and remote Onegin, who has suddenly come into her well-ordered life and turned it totally upside down. This young woman, so full of repressed longing, is incapable of duplicity; she is, in every sense, a virgin, and in the letter she entrusts her heart to Onegin. Anyone who has ever felt the grip of mad passion, and put pen to paper to express it, will know exactly how she feels, how excited and vulnerable she is.

I should note here that *Onegin* is not a typical opera in that neither of the leads ends up committing suicide because the object of his/her affections doesn't or can't respond in kind. (That's *Werther* by Massenet.) Or that one of them is killed by a jealous spouse or lover or lover wannabe. (That's just about every other opera, especially Italian opera.) No, both principal parties survive in *Onegin*—survive in misery, with the horrible realization that what might have been can now never be.

For, incredibly, the blasé playboy spurns Tatiana; country life bores this city lad, and she's only a silly country girl. "If I had wished to pass my life within the confines of the family circle," he tells her, "and a kindly fate had decreed for me the role of husband and father, then, most likely, I would not choose any other bride than you. But I was not made for wedded bliss." Thanks a lot.

Years later, when he meets her again as the Princess Gremina at a ball in St. Petersburg, Onegin realizes why his existence has been so unhappy all these years—killing his best friend Lensky in a duel hasn't helped his quality of life—and now writes *her* a letter. This time, it's her turn to spurn him; she's a married lady now, her husband, the prince, dotes on her. Who can say what might have been? The opera's last image is that of the wiser-but-sadder Onegin, hat in hand, lamenting the hash he has made of things.

All of these developments are adumbrated in the Letter Scene; those with an ear to hear can appreciate how expertly Tchaikovsky realizes Tatiana's uninhibited passion—the music clutches at the listener's heart so forcefully that one is almost embarrassed to witness Tatiana's agonies. "Don't do it!" we want to shout. "He'll only break your heart." But she falls for him anyway.

When she's finished the letter, the orchestra thunders forth with her main theme, punctuating every word she has written. And then the dawn breaks, and we hear the jaunty tune of a shepherd's pipe in the distance, as indifferent to Tatiana's tremendous emotional rite of passage as Onegin will be in the very next scene. It's a brilliant masterstroke, and sums up perfectly the way opera functions on a deeper level than any other art.

The role of music in opera, in other words, is not merely to supply the vehicle by which the action takes place. It does that quite well, and the number of famous tunes from operas is legion. But music also does more: it comments on the dramatic situation from the perspective of third-person omniscience, sometimes sympathetically, sometimes ironically. In order to achieve this effect in the theater you would need to have a commentator standing in the wings, tossing out observations whenever he could get a word in edgewise. In opera you have the commentator sitting in the orchestra pit, and he never shuts up. You just have to pay attention.

Which leads us to another advantage opera has over the theater: the ability to have several conversations going on at once. Try this in a play and you've got the Tower of Babel; the ear simply cannot distinguish among so many words simultaneously. You can prove this for yourself, the next time you are in a large group. When the conversation splits in two, as it eventually does, try to follow both dialogues at the same time. Yes, you can switch back and forth, but to hear and understand every word is impossible.

In opera, it's not. The medium of music makes it possible. In fact, opera goes further: in opera, it's possible to follow four (a quartet), five (a quintet), or six (a sextet) monologues simultaneously—even interior monologues, in which the person is only thinking. Take the great sextet in Act III of Mozart's *The Marriage of Figaro.* Each of the characters on stage is in the grip of a strong emotion. Born out of wedlock, Figaro has just learned the identity of his parents, Dr. Bartolo and Marcellina, who stand revealed, and somewhat embarrassed, before him. The count, who was hoping to make Figaro marry Marcellina to pay off an old debt (and thus make it possible for him to have the delicious Susanna, Figaro's fiancée, to himself), is angry because this is obviously now impossible. The lawyer, Don Curzio, is understandably baffled. Meanwhile, Susanna comes running in with money and finds Figaro in Marcellina's arms, and it is only when the whole affair is explained that she joins in the fun.

Pretty complicated, huh? Not in opera, and not in the hands of a master like Mozart. Even if you don't understand a word of Lorenzo Da Ponte's Italian-language text, it doesn't matter, for the composer guides the listener through the intricacies of the various relationships so seamlessly, so affectionately, that not only is it clear what's going on, it's also clear how we are supposed to feel about it. Mozart has left us a guide to his characters' feelings right there in the music.

And that, in the end, is what makes opera so great. Opera is a window into the soul, which allows us to examine the personality and motivations, the innermost thoughts and dreams, of the characters in a way given to no other art form except the novel. When we look at a painting we can only guess at what might be going on in the hearts and minds of the subjects. Can Cranach's Lucretia really be killing herself with so much equanimity? Is Rubens really as pleased with himself and his bride as their portrait suggests? And just what is the Mona Lisa smiling about, anyway? Emotional ambiguity is one of painting's great strengths and attractions, but the answer to our implied questions will forever be silence.

A movie can go a little deeper into motivation and thought. Even though he is dead at the beginning of the movie, William Holden's character in Billy Wilder's film *Sunset Boulevard* is perfectly able to speak to us, in order to tell us the story of how he died. That, however, requires a tiresome device known as a voice-over, which I personally find invariably jarring. Think of the famous movies that employ it: Coppola's *Apocalypse Now,* Scorsese's *Goodfellas* and *The Age of Innocence,* Ridley Scott's *Blade Runner.* Scott couldn't wait to get rid of Harrison Ford's flat narration when it came time for him to release his director's-cut version of the cult film, and there is little doubt that *Apocalypse Now* would have been better minus Martin Sheen's voice and, indeed, very presence. However essential, voice-overs almost always slow things down and divert attention from the filmmaker's primary responsibility, which is to tell a story with moving pictures; a movie, after all, is not a lecture.

Opera, as I've noted above, doesn't need a narrator because it already has one. Everybody in an opera is a player, including the orchestra. But it is given to the orchestra to be able to do two things at once: to provide the musical underpinning for the singers (they'd sound pretty silly all by themselves up there) and to comment on the action through musical means.

Mine may be a minority view, but years of experience have taught me that the best way to understand opera is to get at it through the music and not the lore or lure of the sets, stage direction, costumes, or singers. After all, singers come and go—if you listen to any opera fan over fifty, you'll get the impression that they mostly go—conductors are variously prized or vilified. The music, however, endures.

And endures and endures. When we talk about opera, we're talking about an art form with a history that is four hundred years old. As the arts go, this is not antiquity; literature is far older, as is the theater, whose repertoire extends back to the ancient Greeks. (Opera, as we'll see later, came about in part through the Renaissance intellectuals' attempt to recapture something of the spirit of Greek theater, which blended poetry and music.) And painting is at least as old as the cavemen, er, cavepersons.

Still, it's a pretty fair chunk of history we're considering here. Which is why I think it's important we go into this with a very clear understanding of what opera can be, what it is supposed to be, and what, at its best, it is.

The point is that no matter what your background, opera is for you, too. Far from being a social butterfly, the true opera fan is in for the music, for the world of experience that opera can give to him. The real opera fan is not satisfied with a steady diet of *Bohème* and *Tosca;* the true opera fan does not live to spend her nights sitting around discussing the relative merits of Callas and Tebaldi with other nerds, digging out old recordings to prove a point. That's the kind of behavior that gives opera a bad name; that's what opera isn't.

On the contrary, the true opera fan is always open to new experience; has well-developed tastes but is willing to be convinced should new evidence come along; and is always on the lookout for new or unusual works that enlarge and expand the repertoire—and in so doing, enlarge and expand our appreciation of what it means to be alive. The true opera fan loves Mozart for his sympathetic insights, Verdi for his humanity, Puccini for his lubricious, unadulterated passion, and Wagner for his courage to hold up the darkest and most perverse secrets of the heart and make us see that we all harbor them.

My theory of the nature of opera may not be original with me—and people have been arguing about the fabulous beast practically from the day it was born—but I came to it on my own. Growing up at various U.S. Marine Corps posts around the country as I did, I had little or no chance to encounter opera as a boy. In fact, I didn't see my first opera—which, if memory serves, was a performance of *Pagliacci* with Franco Corelli, on tour with the Met—until I was well into my teens and living in the Washington, D.C., area. The second opera I saw, Prokofiev's *The Love for Three Oranges,* I was in.

Yes, in. At the Eastman School of Music in Rochester, New York, where I went to college, opera was not part of the curriculum for composers. I suppose that Eastman officials, like almost everybody else at the time, figured that the only good opera composer was a dead opera composer, so why bother? Besides, the mid-1960s were the high-water mark of the twelve-tone school in the groves of academe and, by and large, dodecaphonism and opera just didn't mix. In *Lulu,* Berg had proved that in the right hands they could, but in those days the opera's third act still lay unheard in the composer's archives, and it was not until the late seventies that Berg's great masterpiece could be appreciated in all its glory. We were all learning to write not like Berg, but like Schoenberg, like Webern, like Boulez, like Charles Wuorinen (the old serious Wuorinen, not the frisky Wuorinen of today) and all the other radical serialists in vogue at the time.

The opera department at Eastman, while active, seems in retrospect to have been very much a lesser part of the school. Unless you were a voice major or singing in the chorus, you almost never came in contact with it. My one onstage operatic adventure came about when the school chorus was dragooned into the Prokofiev; I think I played the part of one of the (Kennedy-assassination buffs, please note) Umbrella Men who storm around in the piece's first moments demanding a real opera instead of the fairy tale that ensues and then mercifully disappear.

At Eastman, in fact, singers were considered by the rest of us to be—how shall I put this?—not quite musicians. Instead, they were widely and, in retrospect, snobbishly regarded as vain, silly creatures who placed more importance on looking smart than on having good chops. ("Chops" being the musician's term for technical ability.) The voice majors, especially the girls, would come down to breakfast with not a hair out of place, makeup just so, dressed to kill.

Even when you couldn't see them, you could hear them. A singer testing his or her voice for the first time each day warms up by making a sound like someone falling off a cliff, hitting a medium high note and then swooping rapidly downward to the bottom of the range. Something like this:

Ahh Ahh Ahh
h h h
h h h
h h h
h h h
h h h
h h h
h h h
h h h

This is the equivalent of cold-booting your computer, a kind of vocal diagnostics test to make sure everything is in working order. So there would be all these good-looking folks, bright-eyed and bushy-tailed at seven o'clock in the morning, parading around in their finery and making strange, hawklike noises in their throats. No wonder the rest of us thought they were a little weird.

And not very bright. This is, I know today, a canard, a calumny, an insult, and a damn lie. Nevertheless, it seemed true at the time. On the Eastman School of Music Evolutionary Scale (pat. still pending), the hierarchy of musical types looked like this:

Composers and musicologists
Pianists
Violinists and cellists
Flutists and violists
Clarinetists, oboists, bassoonists
Double-bass players and percussionists
Brass players:
  Trumpeters
  Tubists
  Trombonists
[empty space]
[empty space]
[empty space]
[empty space]
Singers.

The point is, we didn't have much contact with singers, and they didn't have much contact with the rest of the school. Until the day when you, as a composer, had to round up one or two to perform your new song cycle. Why then, you couldn't be nicer, or have more respect for singers. Which I soon did.

My friend Julia, for example. In addition to being a fine soprano, she was an excellent pianist who could accompany herself as she learned her roles, and was game to try anything. If there was one thing she couldn't stand, it was people who said singers were stupid.

"Why don't you try it?" was the challenge she issued one

day to an uppity instrumentalist. "Why don't you try to memorize every note you play"—orchestral musicians never play from memory—"while moving around a stage? Why don't you try not only to memorize every note, but to know your part in two or three different keys, and be ready to transpose at a moment's notice? Why don't you try to play while wearing several pounds of makeup and stitched into a costume? Try that, and then come and tell me singers are stupid."

I had to admit, she had a point. For not only do singers have to know all their roles by heart—can you imagine Musetta reading from the score in the middle of Act II of *La bohème?*—they have to know them in a variety of languages as well: Italian, German, English, French, and Russian. At least they did then: today, with the near-universal acceptance of projected surtitles, one is far less likely to encounter Mozart in English than twenty years ago. A singer's repertoire, however, is not bounded by nationality but by vocal type, or *Fach,* to use the German term that everybody employs, and music for, say, a tenor comes in all national shapes and sizes, from Puccini to Mussorgsky.

When I left Rochester to join the staff of the *San Francisco Examiner* in 1977, I was leaving a city of symphonic and chamber music for one whose passion was opera. And I do mean passion. The San Francisco Opera, under the late Kurt Herbert Adler, had become one of the country's greatest houses, and everyone in don't-call-it-Frisco, it seemed, was an opera fan. The announcement of the fall season is eagerly awaited each year, and when opening night arrives, the city puts on the dog and goes to town. Straight and gay, young and old, rich and semirich, they gather at the War Memorial Opera House on Van Ness Avenue for the traditional Friday-night opening festivities, then repair to Golden Gate Park the following Sunday afternoon for the traditional Opera in the Park free concert. The news media goes wild; it is at once the musical and social Event of the season, annually confirming San Francisco in its high opinion of itself.

So I knew that if I were to do my job, I had better be up to the task. Accordingly, I pored over the score and the libretto to each of the operas scheduled for performance that first season. One of them, I recall, was Verdi's *Don Carlos,* a long, flawed, but magnificent work that poses particular problems for performer and critic alike in that it exists in different four- and five-act forms, different editions, and even different languages.

I read everything I could about *Don Carlos,* including and especially the critic Andrew Porter's researches into the score, during the course of which he discovered much music that Verdi had composed for the opera's premiere in Paris, but cut before the first performance and had never published. By the time *Don Carlos* rolled around my first season, I was ready for it.

My time in San Francisco also provided me with a memorable insight into the psychology of the opera singer. The occasion, which happened to be opening night, was a new production of Ponchielli's *La Gioconda,* starring Luciano Pavarotti and Renata Scotto. Or maybe we should make that, starring Scotto and Pavarotti; it was my billing that got me into trouble.

Scotto sang the opera, but bowed out of the Golden Gate Park concert, which left Pavarotti as the headliner. The *Examiner,* which sponsored the free event, doesn't have its own Sunday edition, and the Saturday version of any newspaper is a pale imitation of its weekday self, so we went big on Friday afternoon with our opera package—featuring, naturally, Pavarotti's appearance in both *Gioconda* and Opera in the Park.

Just before *Gioconda* began, I was approached in the opera house's press room by one of the opera's public relations staff. "Signor Soandso would like to see you," she whispered apologetically. She took me by the hand and led me into the hallway, where I was introduced to a fine-looking Italian gentleman whose name I missed but whose profession—Renata Scotto's husband—soon became clear.

"There's only one star in *La Gioconda*!" he shouted at me, "and thatsa"—he really did say "thatsa"—"La Gioconda!" Having delivered himself of this stunning syllogism, he went on to repeat it several times for my benefit, until even the dumbest Irishman (in this case, me) could figure out that he was shouting about the play Pav got in the paper that afternoon at the expense of the Gioconda herself, Madama Scotto. I muttered some vague words of assurance, excused myself, and headed for my seat. And with the cool professionalism for which I am justly renowned, I didn't even hold it against her when I sat down to write my review later that evening.

When I came to *Time* magazine in 1981, then, I was ready for anything. *Time,* like most magazines, is heavily picture-driven, which is to say that a story with strong illustration possibilities generally has a better chance of getting in the makeup than one without. The managing editor in those days, the brilliant, saturnine Ray Cave, was just beginning to shove the magazine into the era of all color, and in all the sections he demanded the best pictures money could buy. During the Cave years all the editors spent hours screening and selecting pictures to present to the boss, and while a story was always sold on its own merits, the fact that it had good pix to go with it certainly never hurt.

Opera, as you may imagine, has better picture possibilities than, say, symphonic music. Seen one orchestra, seen 'em all; a hundred penguins with musical instruments commanded by some little European fella waving a skinny stick. But opera! Costumes! Sets! Spectacle! *Time* was not only opera-ready, it was opera-friendly.

It also didn't hurt that the company's editor in chief, the top editorial position in what used to be Time Inc., was Henry Anatole Grunwald, himself a former managing editor of *Time.* Grunwald had emigrated along with his family from Vienna to New York as a young boy; back in the old country, his father had been an operetta librettist for the likes of Emmerich Kálmán, and Grunwald retained a love of music, and especially opera, throughout his career. When I was being interviewed for the job, a number of my future colleagues stopped by to say hello.

"You poor son of a bitch," was the unanimous sentiment.

"Why?" I asked.

"Let's put it this way," they said, to a man. "The *Time* music department has one of the highest rates of turnover on the magazine for a reason. You've got one of the toughest senior editors on the staff in Martha Duffy, who eats young writers like you for breakfast. She's a ballet fan, an opera buff, and probably knows more about your subject than you do. The other cultural senior editor, Christopher Porterfield, is a former clarinetist and arranger and, indeed, the former music critic of this magazine, so don't think you're going to get away with anything with him. Then you've got a managing editor, Cave, who couldn't seem to care less about culture and probably wakes up each morning wondering why he has to have the damn stuff in his magazine. So good luck trying to get your stories in the book with any regularity."

"Gee," I said, or words to that effect.

"Finally," the collective colleagues would say, "you've got an editor in chief who cares passionately about music, who is a personal friend of Beverly Sills, and who will read every word you write so critically and take it so personally that you're going to wish you'd never been born when those memos signed HAG start raining down from the thirty-fourth floor."

I took the job anyway and here I am, thirteen years later.

Cave questioned my judgment (to my face, at least) only once, and of course it had to do with opera. Now, you need to understand that, especially in those days, the managing editor of *Time* was like God: omnipotent, omniscient, and omnipresent, and Cave was about as terrifying an apparition as could be imagined. In story conferences, senior editors would cringe whenever he would stroke his beard and cast a basilisk glare at them for one inanity or failure or another.

One day I got word from his secretary that Cave wanted to see me. I had been hearing rumblings that the boss wanted to do a cover story on the New Zealand–born soprano Kiri Te Kanawa, whom he had apparently met at a tennis match; when my opinion on the worthiness of such an idea was solicited, I rejected it.

So there I was, in the Presence. "What's this I hear about you not wanting to do a cover on Kiri Te Kanawa?" asked Cave in his Tidewater accent. His voice, as it always was until he got mad, was low and controlled.

I explained politely that while Ms. Te Kanawa was certainly a leading soprano of her time, I felt there were other musical personalities more worthy of the honor of being on the cover of *Time.*

Cave replied by pointing out the nonmusical facets of Te Kanawa's interesting life—her half-Maori parentage, her adoption by another mixed-race couple, her sensational London debut, etc.

I countered by observing that I personally was not terribly fond of her singing, that in my opinion her lack of a strong musical foundation was a crippling interpretative handicap, and that experience showed that, unable to fall back on the score for sustenance and inspiration, she generally got worse in a role instead of better. And then I shut up.

Cave fixed me with the death stare. Lowly associate editors were supposed to roll over and play dead, not stand up on their hind legs. "All right," he said, his voice slowly rising. "All right. But you'd . . . better . . . be . . . goddamn sure that we're not missing a good story here!" And that was the last I heard about a Kiri Te Kanawa cover.

Of course, he never did run my cover story on Philip Glass.

Chapter 

How to Listen to an Opera, or It Really Isn't as Bad as It Sounds

Modern music, a language a thousand times richer than the language of words, is to speech what thought is to utterance; it arouses sensations and ideas in their primitive form, in that part of us where sensations and ideas have their birth, but leaves them as they are in each of us. That power over our innermost being is one of the grandest facts in music.

—HONORÉ DE BALZAC

A Song that is well and artificially made cannot be well perceived nor understood at the first hearing, but the oftner you shall heare it, the better cause for like you will discover: and commonly that Song is best esteemed with which our Eares are most acquainted.

—WILLIAM BYRD, ENGLISH COMPOSER (1543–1623)

Opera, n. A play representing life in another world, whose inhabitants have no speech but song, no motions but gestures and no postures but attitudes.

—AMBROSE BIERCE, *THE DEVIL'S DICTIONARY*

From the beginning of operatic history until about forty years ago, the way most everybody enjoyed opera was to go to the opera house, buy a ticket, take a seat, and pay attention. Sounds simple enough, and by and large it was. One's operatic expertise was pretty much limited to the number of performances one had seen, and even the most dedicated operagoer (or theatergoer, or concertgoer) could only see so many performances in the course of a lifetime. Verdi not only did not expect that you would become an aficionado of, say, *Un giorno di regno,* he would have been astonished if you had heard it twice—maybe even once—in your life.

For opera, like all other forms of music before the advent of recordings, was meant to be more or less disposable: performed once (or, more exactly, given one run of performances) and then thrown away. On to the next opus! Wagner, probably the most egotistical, solipsistic composer who ever lived, admonished his legion of acolytes, who were circling the Great Man even before the body was cold, to "make something new." He meant this in two ways. One: don't just imitate me, write something different, something that reflects your own voice. And two: keep on chooglin'. Wagner may have consciously intended each of his music dramas to be an enduring masterpiece (well, perhaps not *Die Feen* and *Das Liebesverbot*), to be studied as long as men and women shall stage opera, but he was also remarkably productive. During the course of his nearly seventy years on this planet, Wagner not only composed thirteen operas, most of which are of formidable length and proportions, he also wrote all his own librettos, as well as dozens of pamphlets, books, articles. In addition, he found time to carry on various love affairs, become involved in the disastrous German political uprising of 1848, run an opera house or two, build his own Festival Theater, travel around Europe, and generally keep busy. (Once, in conversation with the brilliant British polymath Jonathan Miller, whose own purview extends from medicine to writing to directing, I wondered aloud how Wagner and the other nineteenth-century geniuses accomplished so much. "They didn't waste their time watching television," he replied.)

Back then, no one could have imagined that someday otherwise perfectly sensible people would sit around arguing whether Adelina Patti in her prime was greater than Joan Sutherland in hers, or whether Gigli really might have been superior to Enrico Caruso, Luciano Pavarotti, and Placido Domingo, and whether maybe, just maybe, the Swede Jussi Björling was the greatest Italian tenor of them all. Fans of the day *did* have their favorite singers, and the opera claque, a group of fans whose zero-sum-game view of the operatic universe meant there could be no success for their favorite without a corresponding disaster for his or her rivals, was an entrenched institution. Crowned heads and titles often attended the opera either in the company of their mistresses (some opera houses, such as the Paris Opéra, even had special antechambers attached to the boxes so that when Cupid called, the demands of Amore could be satisfied privately and discreetly—and you could still catch the third act), or with their opera glasses trained on the heaving breasts and swelling bosoms of their beloveds upon the stage. Meanwhile, the hoi polloi savored the latest tunes, admired the scenery, and debated, often lustily, the merits of both composer and performers.

But to be able to compare singers from vastly different eras had to wait until our own time. And it is no accident that the rise in "singerology" corresponds almost exactly with the rise of the long-playing record and the precipitous—if, thankfully, temporary—decline of the opera as a living art form, both of which occurred just after World War II. Indeed, it has been only in the past decade or so that new operas have begun to win favor with a broad public again; and, naturally, there are complaints that the current vocal talent cannot hold a candle to the stars of the most recent vocal golden age, which ended roughly in the mid-sixties. (This ignores both Pavarotti and Domingo, both of whom rose to prominence in the seventies, but nobody ever said opera fans were consistent.)

This, then, is as good a place as any to dispose of one of the most pernicious myths about opera—that it is about singers. Canary-fancying (as the obsession with singers is sometimes called) is not only *not* the point of going to the opera, it actively hinders the enjoyment thereof. I know of no true opera fan who goes to the Metropolitan primarily to cheer on his or her favorite singer. Such people may appear to be aficionados or connoisseurs, but they're not; no matter how well or poorly their favorite sings, they are going to act in the same embarrassing way, ruining the dramatic and musical progression of the evening with their selfish desire to show off.

In fact, not so very long ago, demonstrations were actually organized ahead of time. The demonstrators were organized into claques and assigned to boo or cheer a certain singer on stage. Callas, for example, had her claques, and her great rival, Renata Tebaldi (for the record, a much better singer and a much worse actress), had hers. When Rudolf Bing, amid much fanfare, unceremoniously fired Callas from the Met in 1958 over a contract dispute, he quietly tried to pave her way back by organizing claques to boo her replacement!

Which brings us back to the question with which we opened this chapter: how do we listen to an opera? And what do we listen for?

As we've seen, opera is a multifaceted theatrical form

made up of elements of music, drama, dance, and design. There are many places to which to direct one's attention, but it is primarily the musical aspect that we are concerned with here, since music (as we've also seen) is the engine that drives the show.

When we're listening to opera on the radio or on recordings, then clearly it is the music that engages the senses. The art form is stripped of its visual component; bereft of scenery and costumes, it stands alone, naked, before the listener. Much as we all agree that opera is a synthesis of the arts, there is no question that, today, it is primarily as music that it reaches its largest audiences.

There is some debate over whether listening to opera on recordings is really "opera" at all, but for our purposes the question is no longer moot. Millions of people experience opera almost exclusively as audio, not video, through the weekly live Met broadcasts that have been winning new adherents for decades and from the widespread availability of CDs.

This is where you'll most likely begin, too. Granted, it can be intimidating walking into the classical section of a record store and picking your first opera out of what seems like the world's largest hat. There are scores of recordings of hundreds of operas, but don't let that stop you. One of the saddest stories I've heard was that of a British acquaintance, who told me that he wanted to learn to like opera but that when he went into a record shop, he was made to feel so out of place by the snooty salesman that he walked out, never to return. So march smartly up to the salesman and either ask for help and get it, or take your business elsewhere. Most classical salesmen, however, are only too happy to win another convert and will usually bend over backward to steer you to an opera you can handle.

Even better, know what you want. Chapter 5 of this book will give you a number of suggestions about where to begin, although soon enough you'll be striking out on your own. In the end, however, there's no trick: listen to the opera and decide whether or not you like it. If you do, great; if not, try another until you either find one that speaks to you or decide this opera stuff is not for you. There's never any need to feel ignorant or stupid when it comes to opera; like wine connoisseurship, it is just a matter of time and experience (and, yes, cash), not any innate or inbred talent or predilection.

Remember, though, that opera on disk is projected entirely through the sounds of the human voice and the orchestra. In the theater, we have the acting of the singers, the sets, the costumes, the choreography, etc., to complement and enhance the music—or, to look at it another way, to be complemented and fulfilled by the music. But on radio or records, opera demands the utmost concentration and study when you're just beginning.

Concentration? Study? In an age of ten-minute attention spans? (Actually, attention spans are probably even shorter now, thanks to the remote control and the phenomenon of "channel surfing"—ten-second attention spans are more like it.)

You'll have to do your homework. There's no substitute for it. If you're new to opera, read the libretto, read some critical commentary, including your local newspapers' reviews if you're going on a second night, get a friend to explain to you what's going on—anything so that you don't approach it cold. There is no better way to learn to hate opera for life than by walking into, say, *Die Meistersinger von Nürnberg* by Wagner without having the slightest idea that it's (a) long, (b) set in medieval Franconia, (c) sung in German, and (d) supposed to be funny. As you sit there, utterly mystified at David's apprentice song, you'll hear the forced guffaws of those in the crowd who, if not fluent in German, at least know where the laugh lines are supposed to be, and you'll pass through various stages of bafflement, hostility, and anger until, at last, another opera hater is born.

So don't do that. Do this instead:

Pick an opera. I'm not going to insult your intelligence or taste by advising you to pick something conventionally tuneful (e.g., *La bohème, La traviata*) or otherwise undeniably Italian. Start with anything you like, as long as it appeals. If you're interested in German culture, give Wagner or Weber a go; if it's melody you want, go for Puccini or Verdi; a Francophile might want to start with Massenet, a Russophile with Mussorgsky or Tchaikovsky. It doesn't matter. Just start with an artifact from a culture you don't already despise.

Read up. Libretto, reviews, books, commentary. Once you begin getting into opera, you'll find an enormous amount of helpful material to guide you through its mazes. And, in fact, the deeper you get into opera the more you're going to want to know about it, so don't be surprised if, some time after your first exposure to *Bohème,* you're not only singing along with Rodolfo or Mimi but you're reading biographies of Puccini and checking out Murger (the French author on whose novel the book is based) in translation from the library. The path from novice to expert in opera is not very long.

Listen up. You may be able to enjoy Prince (although I have no idea how, or why) by listening with only one ear, or half your brain, but opera is sterner stuff, and it demands that you pay it full and complete attention. Knowing the libretto, then, is not incidental to your enjoyment of the piece, it's crucial. Since the music is almost completely context-driven, it's important to know what, dramatically, is going on while the orchestra is raging, or going *rum-tum-tum.* Knowing the dramatic situation—where you are in the piece—is indispensable to appreciating the music in all its glory, not just in all its tunefulness.

Which is why, in the end, opera is not about melody. For all its ravishing melodic moments, opera must be fashioned out of something sturdier in order for it to carry the burden of dramatic action and narrative for two, three, or four hours.

Let's start by taking an example from a world that

might be more familiar: Broadway. When people complain about the lack of "hummable-mummable melodies" in the work of a composer like Sondheim, for example, what, exactly, are they complaining about? To paraphrase Mark Twain, Sondheim's music is neither as bad as it sounds, nor as sophisticated as the *New York Times*'s invariably unmusical drama critics think it is. What it is, is a supporting framework for the composer-lyricist's dazzling word play, in which the arias are constructed along the same lines as the recitatives (a sort of sung speech), which is why it takes a brilliant arranger such as Jonathan Tunick to make it come alive.

In this constructive sense, Sondheim's music is quintessentially "operatic"—far more so than Andrew Lloyd Webber's, which is often accused of being "operatic" (as if that were a sin in a venue that has seen the world premieres of George Gershwin's *Porgy and Bess* and Leonard Bernstein's *Candide*). Webber is a far more accomplished tunesmith than Sondheim, and in works like *The Phantom of the Opera* and *Aspects of Love*—not to mention *Jesus Christ Superstar* and *Evita,* both of which are called operas by the composer—he spins out tune after tune after tune, with no reliance on spoken dialogue and precious little recitative, which is Sondheim's stock in trade. Instead, Webber composes his non-aria material in a semituneful way, often with echoes or forecasts of the show's big melodies, which makes it appear to the ignorant that his musicals are nothing but a series of unrelated melodies strung together.

So which is the real "opera" composer? The answer is: both. It is probably only in the late twentieth century that we would even ask such a question, or think of separating "pop" from "high" culture. Verdi was no ivory-tower egghead, but a passionately popular composer who wrote with the audience in mind; Mozart aimed *The Magic Flute* directly at what we might consider today a "Broadway" audience, just as Bernstein did a couple of centuries later with *West Side Story* (story by W. Shakespeare, lyrics by S. Sondheim, by the way). When Webber says *Sunset Boulevard* is an opera, should we believe him? When Sondheim's biographer, Martin Gottfried, says the composer writes shows, not operas, should we believe him? What is the difference, anyway?

In other words: how do we listen to opera?

Here we go again. We listen by first understanding what the role of music is, *so we know what to listen to and for.* The big arias, or tunes, will come and go, but if you sit around looking at your watch, waiting impatiently for "Di quella pira" from *Il trovatore* by Verdi, and thinking everything else inferior or boring, you're going to be pretty unhappy. (*"Parsifal,"* quipped one wag, "is the kind of opera that starts at six o'clock. After it has been going three hours you look at your watch and it says six-twenty." That's the wrong way to listen.) But if you understand that the opera's entire score is, especially after the middle of the nineteenth century, a more or less seamless structure designed to deliver the music-drama in the most striking and efficient way possible, then you will be able to endure the longest, most arid stretches of operatic recitative with a smile on your lips and a song in your heart.

But what about arias, duets, trios, quartets, ensembles, choruses, etc.? Shouldn't a discussion of how to listen to opera tell us what all these mysterious things are? Surely, there's more to opera than understanding the function of the music.

Well, yes. But not much more.

Once you understand your first opera, you're well on your way to understanding them all; the key is to know what makes them tick, how they're put together. But if we were to make a gross generalization (is there another kind?), we might break down opera, especially eighteenth- and nineteenth-century opera, into the following two components:

1) Arias, duets, and other moments of Big Melody that declaim the big emotions, the internal struggles, and the passionate feelings of the main characters, including the chorus, which often functions as a single entity.
2) Recitative, *Sprechstimme,* and other song-speech devices (including Wagner's "endless melody," which of course isn't) that move the story along until it's time to call a time-out, and have an aria, duet, etc.

And that's about it; as Ross Perot might say, it's that simple.

To put opera back into its theatrical context, think of "recit" as the dialogue of a play, the repartee between and among characters, the author's delivery mechanism of his plot. The arias and ensembles, on the other hand, are the speeches, the monologues, that allow us to peer inside the character's head and heart. Duets and the larger ensembles, right up to octets, offer us the opportunity to get to know multiple characters simultaneously, allowing the composer to heighten and intensify the relationships in a way denied a mere playwright.

So recits are about plot; arias are about emotions.

Okay, okay, you say: I know all about arias. They're what Pavarotti sings at soccer games. But what is this recit stuff?

It's the abbreviation of the word *recitative* (pronounced "re-che-ta-TEEVE"). Early operas consist almost entirely of recit (inconsistently, we say "reh-sit" when we shorten the word), which made sense, given the primacy of the words at that time. By the time we get to Handel and Mozart, though, arias and ensembles have become far more prominent, which is why some people get the idea that you have to suffer through the recit vegetables in order to get the arias for dessert.

Ahh, but you already know that's not true. You already understand how music underlines the drama, how scores by geniuses like Mozart, Verdi, Puccini, and Wagner have an internal unity and cohesion that add up to more than the sum of their parts, that you can't have an opera made up exclusively of arias. So think of the recits as the bridges between arias and ensembles, the connective tissue that binds an eighteenth-century opera together. They are the sinews that allowed composers like Mozart to achieve an unprecedented psychological flexibility in their writing, and to bring to life such diverse, and deeply human characters, as Figaro, Don Giovanni, Fiordiligi and Dorabella, Tamino and Pamina.

Now, about those arias . . .

They're not just what Pavarotti sings at soccer games. Nor are they merely the "greatest hits" from each opera, the tunes the fans have been waiting for, patiently enduring those darn recits until they get to the good stuff. The arias, and their larger cousins, the ensembles and choruses, are the emotional centers of opera, the moments when the characters get to tell us how they feel about what is going on. It's easy to make fun of the worst excesses of arias—the ten-minute death scenes, in which the tenor or soprano pours out his or her soul while endlessly expiring—but folks who point to the "unreality" of such scenes simply don't know what they are talking about. And here's why:

As we've seen, opera is essentially about understanding emotions through the preternatural medium of music. When Tristan spends the first half of Act III of Wagner's *Tristan und Isolde* dying from the wounds he received in his fight with Melot, he is of course suffering physically. (You would be, too, if you'd had a sword run through you.) But, far more important to the meaning of the opera, Tristan is suffering emotionally—suffering from the frustration of his interrupted love scene with Isolde, and suffering even more from her absence. His death is a foregone conclusion—so was Wagner supposed to have him simply drop dead at the end of Act II? Of course not. The raving Tristan must sing before he dies—sing with the clarity born of insanity, sing of his unrequited passion for Isolde, of his fear of the coming of the day, of his love for the night, which embraces and protects him. Without Tristan's long final aria, there is no closure to his character: he *must* stay alive long enough for Isolde to join him at his castle in Brittany, for him to breathe one last breath and collapse dead in her arms.

Just as important is Isolde's final scene (the famous "Liebestod," or "Love Death"). She, too, has unfinished business; she, too, must resolve her feelings not only toward Tristan but toward her husband, King Marke, as well. This she does in a final "aria" (if such a word can do justice to Wagner's most poetic triumph) that embraces the spectrum of earthly love in a way unequaled before or since. Yes, Isolde sings for a very long time before she sinks slowly to the ground, lifeless; yes, it doesn't make any "sense" for her to die suddenly for no apparent reason. No sense, that is, to an operatic ignoramus. But once we understand the context of the last act of *Tristan,* it makes perfect sense. It is the only possible ending. And it is every bit as "realistic" as a drive-by shooting.

What makes some people so uncomfortable about *Tristan* is not the violent and gloomy action but its alarmingly unambiguous subtext—sex, of course. *Tristan und Isolde* is permeated by sex, and especially by sex in its conjunction with death: Eros and Thanatos, together again. From the revolutionary opening bars of the famous Prelude (which, when combined orchestrally with the "Liebestod," offers the listener a kind of Reader's Digest version of the opera), the scent of a woman is in the air; the Act II love duet is the most explicit depiction of coitus interruptus in musical history. The frustrated orgasm the lovers experience, when their tryst in suddenly adjourned by the arrival of the king, must find an outlet, and that outlet must and does occur at the very end of Act III. There would not be a franker discussion of sexuality in music until Shostakovich's *Lady Macbeth of Mtsensk.*

So now, perhaps, we have arrived at the heart—or

maybe the root—of the matter. However you slice it, so to speak, opera is about sex. Not tawdry, dirty, physical sex, necessarily, although it can be about that too. (James Joyce's *Ulysses* has nothing on, say, Mozart's *Così fan tutte.*) Rather, opera concerns itself with the fundamental facts of our existence on the planet, which is why it is at once so sexy and so violent. Eros and Thanatos, Love and Death. When you strip opera naked, this is what is left. Opera is the most profoundly human art form yet invented.

Chapter 3

A Brief (Don't Worry) History of Opera, or How Did It Get That Way?

I do not mind what language an opera is sung in so long as it is a language I don't understand.

—Sir Edward Appleton in *The Observer*, 1955

The Opéra is nothing but a public gathering place, where we assemble on certain days without precisely knowing why.

—Voltaire

Opera in English is, in the main, just about as sensible as baseball in Italian.

—H. L. Mencken

The operatic repertoire is fundamentally the creation of Dead White European Males, and if you don't like it, tough. The opera house is no place for political correctness (come to think of it, what is?), so I must warn you from the outset that this discussion of opera's origins is irrevocably bound up with culture. To be sure, singing is a universal impulse, and vocal music is found in every society, but for the purposes of this discussion, we will be tracing opera's development from its origins in Renaissance Italy, to its spread across continental Europe and Britain and, finally, to its extension to the Americas. Most of the important figures are male, and most of them white; that's the way it is.

We know that some form of music theater has been around since the ancient Greeks; the plays of Aeschylus, Sophocles, and the others were declaimed to the accompaniment of winds and strings, and the chorus was an integral part of the drama, commenting on the action. Greek theater, so powerful even in the reading today, was a tribal—what we might call a "community"—event of overwhelming power and significance. The Athenians did not attend the theater in order to relax after a busy day inventing philosophy and squabbling with the Spartans. They assembled in their open-air theaters the way eighteenth-century New England Protestants gathered in their houses of worship, as a form of religious ritual that had something important to tell them about how they should, and should not, live their lives.

It is this liturgical quality that, even today, distinguishes opera from the other arts. Painting has long since lost its connection to religion, and nobody makes illuminated manuscripts anymore, but in order to experience an opera, we must make a pilgrimage to the place of worship, take off our hats, and sit quietly during the service. Although we are removed from the Greeks by millennia, the religious resonance lingers on.

In the mid-sixteenth century, when the intellectuals of Europe were rediscovering the humanistic values of Greek civilization by filtering Greek culture through the lens of their own desires, composers and other artists deliberately sought to return to some of the Hellenistic ideals. Opera, which first appeared at the end of the sixteenth century, was thus part of a generalized European cultural revolution against what we have conveniently tagged the Middle Ages, as modern secular Europe began to emerge from the Latin Gothic dominance of the Church.

Musically, the revolt was against the complex, text-obscuring polyphony of the early Renaissance that was threatening to tie music into knots. In such music, the five, six, or even seven voices (whether vocal or instrumental) twined and intertwined so contrapuntally that music was becoming almost too dense to be listened to. It needed clarification, simplification, a return to first principles, which music does every hundred years or so. Indeed, a pendulum swing between simplicity and complexity is one of the hallmarks of music history. Gregorian chant to motets; early opera to baroque opera; the classical style to the late romantic and the twelve-tone school; minimalism and—well, who knows what will follow?

Anyway, along came a man named Jacopo Peri, born in August of 1561, probably in Rome. Like all musicians of the day, he began his career as a singer (tenor) and keyboard player in the churches—in his case, in Florence. Peri's first composition was one of the *intermedi,* or musical numbers between acts of a drama, for Giovanni Fedini's court entertainment, *Le due Persilie* in 1583, and six years later he participated in the big blowout that celebrated the wedding of Grand Duke Ferdinando I de' Medici and Christine of Lorraine. That wedding changed the course of musical—and, for that matter, political—history.

The Medici court gathered to it an extraordinary group of artists and thinkers. One of them was Jacopo Corsi, the city's leading patron of music, who in turn was influenced by the theories of the so-called Florentine camerata led by one Giovanni de' Bardi. Both groups unfavorably compared the state of the arts in their day with what they imagined was the much higher standard that obtained during the classical period of Greece and Rome. Corsi encouraged Peri and the poet Ottavio Rinuccini to reinvent a kind of musical theater the Greeks might have admired, and the fruit of their collaboration was the first opera, *Dafne,* premiered in 1597.

Only bits and pieces of *Dafne* survive (another famous *Dafne,* by Marco da Gagliano, was composed in 1608), some of them written by Corsi, but these are sufficient to demonstrate that a new, simplified, more direct musical style had come into being—something that was made clear in Peri and Rinuccini's next work, *Euridice,* first performed on October 6, 1600, at the Pitti Palace in Florence to celebrate another wedding, that of Maria de' Medici and Henri IV of France. Like *Dafne, Euridice* took its inspiration from Greek mythology. Peri himself sang the title role, but in case you have the idea that he was accompanied by a symphony orchestra à la Verdi or Puccini, the musical accompaniment consisted of a harpsichord (played by Corsi), a chitarrone, a lirone, and a lute.

What do these early operas sound like? You may be disappointed to know that, although they contain arias, choruses, and instrumental interludes, they consist largely of recitatives. There are no "greatest hits" from these early Florentine operas, no arias that pop up on television, no anthems that have found their way into commercials. Instead, they sound almost as if the characters are speaking to us in the rich vowel sounds of the Italian language. The music is fluid and flexible, existing to serve the text and put across the story. (For a chicken-and-egg discussion of the function of words and music in opera, see the next chapter.)

Very quickly, opera got its first great composer and its first great masterpieces. The composer was Claudio Monteverdi, born in Cremona and, at the time of his first opera, *Orfeo* (1607), working in the duke of Mantua's court. (Centuries later, Giuseppe Verdi would make a sixteenth-century duke of Mantua the villain of *Rigoletto.*) *Orfeo* was in part a competitive response to the burgeoning Florentine operatic scene. The lead role was sung by Francesco Rasi, who had also performed in Peri's *Euridice* (where Monteverdi very likely heard him), but otherwise Monteverdi's work marked a distinct advancement over the Florentine school. For one thing, it was explicitly divided into acts (even if they were probably played without a break). But even more important, it wedded the best of the old madrigalian technical complexity with the new ideal of limpid expression to give the fledgling art form a depth and seriousness that won for it a permanent place in European art.

Monteverdi followed *Orfeo* with masterpiece after masterpiece, including *The Combat Between Tancred and Clorinda, The Return of Ulysses* and, especially, *The Coronation of Poppea* (1642), the oldest opera still in the current repertoire. Yes, the patrimony of *Poppea* is in question: some of it, as it has come down to us today, was clearly written by other composers (in fact, the opera was not attributed to Monteverdi until 1681). But with its forward-looking emphasis on tuneful arias, *Poppea* not only pleases modern audiences, it also paved the way for the development of the art form in the baroque period.

By the time of *Poppea,* something else had happened of crucial importance: opera had come out of the royal courts and into the public theaters, the first of which, the Teatro San Cassiano in Venice, opened in 1637. The significance of this cannot be overemphasized, especially when you consider that the institution of the public piano recital, for example, didn't begin until Liszt in the nineteenth century. And here we are, in seventeenth-century Venice, on our way to the opera.

And not just Venice. Opera spread widely and quickly, although in each country it was tailored for local consumption. Sometimes it took and sometimes it didn't: in England one major native opera, *Dido and Aeneas* by Henry Purcell, appeared in 1689, following which the form went underground for almost three hundred years. *Dido,* which contains the famous aria for the heroine, "When I Am Laid in Earth" (and which has given rise to much risible comment among singers ever since), is a real opera, unlike Purcell's other works, which are "semi-operas." In such works as *King Arthur* and *The Fairy Queen,* the composer combined the English passion for the theater with the new techniques of opera. Would that he had lived longer: Purcell died in 1695, at the age of thirty-six or thirty-seven, and England would not see his equal, either as a musician or as a setter of the English language, until Benjamin Britten in the twentieth century.

In France, opera flourished with the coming of the baroque. If the English wanted their operas to be more like plays, the French wanted operas that looked and sounded like ballets. Composers such as André Campra and Marc-Antoine Charpentier perfected the form of the opera-ballet in works like *L'Europe galante* and *Le malade imaginaire.* Later, composers like Lully and Rameau created more sophisticated musical edifices, although their works, like most early French opera, have not really caught on with the wider, non-French public. They seem somehow too precious, too delicate, too *French* for consumption outside their native land and, without prejudice, we will pass over them lightly.

Oddly, the high point of Italian baroque opera took place in England, where it was composed by a German who went by the anglicized name George Frideric Handel. We tend to think of Handel today as the composer of *Messiah* and other oratorios, but he primarily made his career in opera, both as a composer and as a producer. Between 1710 and 1740, Handel dominated the English operatic scene, composing new operas at the rate of more than one a year. Handel was a great synthesizer, adopting and adapting not only the Italian form of opera but also the French and creating a body of work probably unequaled in terms of its quality.

Unfortunately, Handel's operas are now almost wholly out of favor, thanks to the style in which they are written. By the time of Handel, the battle between aria and recitative had been decided in favor of the former, and Handel's operas consist of long, long, *long* stretches of what are called da capo arias. A da capo aria consists of an endless A section, followed by a contrasting but interminable B section, followed by a recapitulation of the A section, at the conclusion of which suicide seems a viable option—on the part of the listeners, that is. Another strike against Handel is the necessity of using castrato singers in the leading roles, of which there are no more; sopranos and countertenors just don't make the same effect. A third strike is Handel's penchant for opera seria, a parade of serious, mythology-based operas that seem stodgy and humorless, especially when compared with the works of Mozart, who was born three years before Handel died.

Handel also suffered from a sea change in the taste of the London public, which was partly occasioned by the infighting and rivalry that went on among the producers of Italian opera. Then as now, opera was something of a shoestring affair, at least as far as profit margins went, and Handel's opera companies were always struggling with debt. The fact that they were for a time extremely fashionable didn't necessarily help; in the fickle world of opera, you could become yesterday's news with alarming speed. Nor did bad management help; one of Handel's administrators at the Queen's Theatre, Haymarket, the aptly named Owen Swiney, fleeced the immigrant a year after Handel had settled permanently in London, absconding with the money in 1713. Handel was named master of the orchestra at the newly established Royal Academy of Music, but its operatic activities went under in 1728, partly due to a fierce battle between the company's two leading ladies, Francesca Cuzzoni and Faustina Bordoni. Rival companies, such as the Opera of the Nobility, sprang up in 1733 and quickly won control of Handel's theater (now called the King's Theatre) in Haymarket, which it held until the company's collapse in 1737.

In the meantime, something else had happened. In 1728, John Rich and John Gay presented the first and best "ballad opera," called *The Beggar's Opera,* and it was a sensation. Using existing English, Irish, and Scots folk tunes—and brazenly helping themselves to a tune from Handel's *Rinaldo*—to support a topical text of pointed political satire, Rich and Gay created a wholly new form of popular opera that seriously dented Handel's increasingly archaic concoctions. Tastes changed; bowing to the inevitable, Handel by 1741 abandoned Italian opera in favor of English oratorio.

So are Handel's operas worth hearing? While I don't recommend them for beginners, in the hands of an audacious director like Peter Sellars, whose Boston production of *Orlando* was set in the space age, they can still hold the stage given enough expertise on the part of the performers and enough patience and goodwill on the part of the audiences. There are zillions of them—*Rinaldo, Teseo, Silla, Radamisto, Ottone, Flavio, Giulio Cesare, Tamerlano, Scipione, Berenice, Serse, Semele,* and many, many more—and you could spend your whole life in the major opera houses of the world and never encounter one. The best way to sample Handel is in small doses, on records, armed with a libretto and, preferably, a score.

Another opera composer honored more in memory than by performance is Christoph Willibald Gluck, who is notable for being the first great operatic reformer, rebelling against the excesses of Handelian opera and attempting to restore the form to its Florentine origins; the music, Gluck felt, should support the text, and not vice versa. We'll discuss Gluck in more detail in the next chapter, but it is worth observing that, like Handel, Gluck was a Germanic composer who achieved his highest fame writing operas in other languages, in his case, French. The nascent German language, which had achieved its standard written form only with Luther's translation of the Bible, was still regarded as inferior to the romance languages, French and Italian, and good Germans who wanted success in the wider world had better learn a civilized language fast.

Which brings us to Mozart. I generally abhor and eschew superlatives when it comes to composers, but I do believe that Mozart was the greatest composer who ever lived, and naturally wrote the greatest operas as well. A famous child prodigy, the Salzburg-born Mozart traveled widely as a boy, learning French and Italian on his travels in those countries and getting as far as England. He was, in other words, an internationalist from the get-go, and the depth and breadth of his experience are evident in every note he wrote.

Mozart wrote, by one count, twenty-one operas, three of which were composed before he was twelve, and six or seven of which not only remain in the repertoire, but form its core. Mozart was a child of his time and wrote his share of opera seria in the Italian style; two of the best are *Mitridate* and *Il sogno di Scipione* (*Scipio's Dream*). The first major opera, *Idomeneo,* still widely performed in our day, was written 1780–81. Like any good opera seria, it takes place in the classical world, in this case Crete after the Trojan War, and while its libretto seems arch and stilted to us, the music is so fresh in conception and so vivid in characterization that it sweeps everything else before it. (Both Pavarotti and Domingo sing this opera, which ought to tell you something.)

And then, in succession, came masterwork after masterwork. *The Abduction from the Seraglio* is a comic German singspiel, or opera with spoken dialogue; *The Marriage of Figaro, Don Giovanni,* and *Così fan tutte* are the three ineffable Italian-language operas to librettos by Lorenzo Da Ponte, works so rich in beauty and insight as to form the base of every other work in the operatic repertoire. Near the end of his life, Mozart turned again to singspiel in *The Magic Flute* and then topped off everything with a valedictory return to opera seria in the formerly underrated (but not anymore) *La clemenza di Tito.* Mozart's contribution to opera is far more than a simple catalogue of standard works or collection of hit tunes. What Mozart did was nothing less than to realize opera's full potential as a mirror of the human condition; everything, and everybody, after him is gravy.

For proof, look at Beethoven. Beethoven wrote one opera, *Fidelio* (although he wrote it several times; in earlier versions it was called *Leonore*), and nothing could illustrate the influence of Mozart more dramatically than this work, conceived just fourteen years after Mozart's death. *Fidelio* is a "rescue opera" of the kind then very much in vogue in Vienna; Luigi Cherubini, an Italian-born composer of French operas and one of Beethoven's influences, wrote several of them. And, of course, the music of the French Revolution was very much in the air, especially with the Napoleonic campaigns raging across Europe.

Fidelio, the story of a political prisoner named Florestan and his wife, Leonore, who disguises herself as the youth Fidelio in order to free him, begins very much in comic-opera style. (There is a subplot about the infatuation of Marzelline, the jailer's daughter, for the in-drag Leonore.) But gradually it turns into something far more serious and universal, a full-fledged romantic opera that, for all its many dramatic difficulties and vocal infelicities, has a secure place on the roster of every opera house in the world. *Fidelio* is a miracle, a magnificent opera by a composer never very comfortable with vocal music, a thrilling ode to love and freedom whose own genesis was so checkered and difficult that a sense of struggle and triumph seems hammered into every note of the score.

With *Fidelio* we are now well and truly into the romantic period, from which comes most of what we think of today as "opera." If Beethoven's masterpiece was influenced by the French composers, they now came into their own once more, led by the formidable figure of Giacomo Meyerbeer, a German-born Jewish composer (his real name was Jakob Liebmann Meyer Beer). Meyerbeer is not much performed today, but in his own time he was the Andrew Lloyd Webber of the music theater. Spectacle was the operative word for Meyerbeer; in such works as *Robert le diable* (1831) and *Les Huguenots* (1836), Meyerbeer tackled huge and fantastic subjects, whose productions were very much the talk of *le Tout-Paris.* So famous was Meyerbeer that a young, ambitious German composer journeyed to Paris to enlist his aid in furthering his fledgling, and up to that point, checkered, career. His name was Richard Wagner.

Wagner is so very much the dominant musical figure of the nineteenth century that he tends to obscure almost everyone else, with the exception of his chief contemporary Giuseppe Verdi. At the height of Meyerbeer's fame, there were also significant operatic developments in Italy—namely, the bel canto school of Gioacchino Rossini, Vincenzo Bellini, and Gaetano Donizetti, which shared with Meyerbeer a love for extravagant vocalism. Rossini's frothy comic operas, such as *The Barber of Seville* (oddly, *William Tell,* perhaps his finest, is very much a serious work), Bellini's exaggerated emotional dramas, such as *Norma* and *I Puritani,* and Donizetti's somewhat abler blend of comic and dramatic elements (*The Daughter of the Regiment, Lucia di Lammermoor*) all maintain firm places in the international repertoire today, although their entertainment value as singers' showpieces is superior to their intrinsic musical quality, if you ask me. This is very much my pet peeve, but I find the bel canto operas, with their simple harmonies and rum-tum orchestral accompaniments, almost wholly devoid of musical interest and a chore to sit through. But you may not.

Which, thankfully, brings us to Wagner and Verdi. Both men were born in 1813, and both dominated the rest of the century (Wagner died in 1883, Verdi in 1901). One was a volcanic revolutionary, whose range of thought—and deed—extended from music and drama to philosophy and politics; the other, owing to his artistic stature, found himself symbolizing the hopes and aspirations of the Italian people in their drive for political unity. Between them, they created the heart of the modern operatic repertoire, reinvented the form twice over, perfected it, and handed it off to the next generation.

Trying to choose between them is impossible, although it was a choice that you practically had to make if you lived during the last century. They appeared to be polar opposites: Wagner, the radical inventor of "The Music of the Future," as opposed to Verdi, the conservator of the Italian vocal tradition. To root for one marked you as either a right-thinking progressive or a dangerous anarchist; to cheer the other signified your utter musical conservatism, or your respect for the creative uses of tradition.

Verdi was a slow starter; of his twenty-eight operas, the first dozen or so remain fairly obscure, being revived more in honor of the later works than through any particular merit of their own. And yet, through this long and painstaking process of musical discovery, Verdi was not only able to create the masterpieces of *Don Carlos* (originally composed in French, for the Paris Opéra, as a kind of Meyerbeerian sensation), *Otello,* and *Falstaff,* he was able to bring his large and devoted audience with him nearly every step of the way. Everybody knows the famous story of Verdi's withholding of the aria "La donna è mobile" from *Rigoletto* until the last minute because he knew that as soon as it was heard in rehearsal, folks would be singing it in the streets. That's how acute Verdi's sense of the popular taste was.

Nobody ever sang Wagner in the streets. (Can you imagine ambling along the boulevards with a merry "Ho-yo-to-ho" on your lips?) His music, composed in a declamatory style that takes some getting used to, saves most of its good tunes for the orchestra. But what Wagner was after was nothing less than the transformation of the operatic form into something that would encompass the entire range of knowledge and experience. If Verdi was the great humanist—and the composer's feelings for his characters are always fully in evidence—Wagner was the great arbiter of the unconscious, probing deeply in the wellsprings of emotion and memory. In his mammoth *Ring of the Nibelung* cycle, he created what was probably the most ambitious single work in the history of art, if we don't count Chartres Cathedral; in the sunny *Die Meistersinger* he looked at love with wisdom and affection, while in the brooding *Tristan,* written at the same time as *Meistersinger,* he explored the darker nature of eroticism. Nobody was, or could be, neutral about Wagner, which is exactly the way he wanted it.

If the race between Verdi and Wagner (a race Verdi certainly did not participate in) was to see who would have the greater influence on the coming twentieth century, then Wagner wins in a walk. From about the middle of the nineteenth century on, the German school came to dominate nearly every creative aspect of music. Up to this point, the Germans had been fairly quiet. Handel, as we saw, made his career in England, writing in the Italian style; Mozart was an Austrian, born and raised in Salzburg, the German-speaking world's most Italianate city. The first prominent composer of wholly German opera was Carl Maria von Weber, one of Wagner's major influences; his *Der Freischütz* (1821), a spooky tale of the supernatural, continues to be popular, especially among German audiences.

After Wagner, however, came the deluge. His most important successor was probably the Bavarian composer Richard Strauss (no relation to the Viennese "Waltz King" family of the same name), who presents an interesting study in reverse motion. Strauss, the son of a famous horn player, first burst on the scene as a composer of brilliant orchestral tone poems—single-movement works of so-called program music, which tell a story. Among them are *Don Juan, Till Eulenspiegel,* and *Ein Heldenleben,* and they remain staples of the orchestral repertoire.

Basically, Strauss wrote almost his entire run of superb tone poems before he struck paydirt with his first major opera, *Salome,* in 1905. (Like Wagner, whose *Die Feen* and *Das Liebesverbot* antedate his first triumph, *Rienzi,* Strauss wrote two earlier works—*Guntram* and *Feuersnot*—that have never quite stuck.) He followed up the shocking *Salome* with the even more powerful *Elektra,* on which he collaborated with Sophocles by way of the librettist Hugo von Hofmannsthal. This was the first Strauss-Hofmannsthal joint venture, a partnership that bore fruit most famously in *Der Rosenkavalier.*

After *Rosenkavalier,* which surely must be judged the high-water mark of romantic opera, the bloom went off the Straussian rose (double-pun alert: the German word *Strauss* means, among other things, "bouquet"). *Ariadne auf Naxos* is certainly very fine, although its German-language spoken dialogue can be rough sledding for those who don't understand it, and *Die Frau ohne Schatten* (*The Woman without a Shadow*) has its moments—as well as its long half hours. After that, though, it was pretty much all downhill for Strauss, operatically speaking (morally, too, since he became the head of the Third Reich's music organization), and most of the rest of the Straussian operatic output is pretty grim—tonal music without melody.

If Strauss is Wagner's most important descendant, then Giacomo Puccini is Verdi's. Puccini has, for some reason, come in for a good deal of critical drubbing in our time, and some drama critics obviously think the adjective "Puccinian" is a term of opprobrium, so often do they apply it to Broadway shows like *Aspects of Love* in order to call attention to the fact that one can actually hum the tunes. But Puccini's abilities as a musician far outstrip his admittedly fabulous gift for melody. Listen to any Puccini score—*La bohème, Tosca, Madama Butterfly, Turandot* to name the most famous—and you will be amazed at his sure-handed technical grasp, his exquisite orchestration, and his all-around good sense in choosing subjects that brought out the best in him; you won't hear me uttering a disparaging word about Puccini in this book. Puccini (along with the one-shot verismo twins Mascagni and Leoncavallo, of *Cav 'n Pag* fame) was the last elevated exponent of Italian opera, and with *Turandot,* which the composer was working on at his death in 1924, the line that began with the Florentine camerata and Peri comes to an end.

A brief word about our old friends, the French. Unlike French wine, French opera tends not to travel, but this period saw the creation of one of the finest and most popular operas of all time, Georges Bizet's *Carmen.* Like *The Magic Flute, Carmen* was composed with spoken dialogue instead of recitatives, which made it somehow not "serious" enough; after the composer's untimely death at thirty-six, it was tricked out with recits by another composer. It is only lately that we have been permitted to hear *Carmen* the way Bizet conceived it between 1873 and 1875.

The other French repertoire masterpiece is Claude Debussy's *Pelléas et Mélisande,* probably the finest wedding of text and music in operatic history. Maeterlinck's recondite drama found its perfect musical realization in Debussy's languid, elliptical music. Not that the two men were anything like friends. The poet clashed with the composer openly over the casting of Mary Garden in the title role—Maeterlinck wanted his mistress to get the part—and went on record as saying he hoped the opera would fail at its premiere in 1902. *Vive la France!*

Before we advance too far into the twentieth century—and Strauss lived until 1949—I should mention a couple of the Slavic national schools. The Russians are best represented by Tchaikovsky, of course, and by Modest Mussorgsky, whose epic *Boris Godunov* is a must for all opera lovers. In sweep and scope it surpasses even Verdi's *Don Carlos,* and few climaxes can rival the death of Czar Boris as he topples from his throne in terror and remorse. The last scene, in which the character of the Fool bewails the fate of Mother Russia, should have been required listening for the Bush and Clinton administration State Department officials who botched the chance to bring the former Soviet Union into the fold of modern nations after its collapse.

The Czechs also developed a formidable domestic opera industry, led by Leoš Janáček, whose first major success, the masterpiece *Jenůfa,* was produced when he was sixty-two years old and brought him "overnight" fame. Janáček was a friend and student of Antonin Dvořák's, whose own *Rusalka* is full of lovely things, and living proof that if you stick with something long enough you'll eventually succeed. Up to *Jenůfa,* a frank and passionate depiction of the fate of an unwed mother in a provincial Moravian village, Janáček wrote almost nothing that is still performed today. After it, he embarked on an astonishingly prolific decade that saw the creation of the operas *Katya Kabanova, The Makropulos Affair* and *From the House of the Dead,* as well as the Sinfonietta and the *Glagolitic Mass.* Each work is composed in Janáček's wholly original style, influenced by the (to our ears) strange cadences of the Czech language and based on an otherworldly sense of harmony that is at once fresh and invigorating.

Which brings us, more or less, to that dreaded creature, twentieth-century opera. Considering that the twenty-first century is almost upon us, there hardly seems any good reason to continue to skulk about in fear of modern music, and yet twentieth-century opera is still considered a money loser and a room emptier by many unenlightened opera company managers, who apparently feel the "ugly" sounds of our century might grate upon the dainty ears of their genteel patrons.

Right. Never mind that both *Der Rosenkavalier* and *Turandot* are twentieth-century operas. No, what they're thinking of is something like Alban Berg's *Wozzeck,* premiered in 1925, just a few months before *Turandot.* We'll discuss both *Wozzeck* and *Lulu* in greater detail in chapter five, but suffice it to say that they are superficially a world removed from the late-romantic musings of Strauss and Puccini. *Wozzeck* is, by and large, atonal, meaning it has no clearly defined home key, while *Lulu* is unquestionably the outstanding example of the twelve-tone system in opera. For these technical reasons, audiences have had a hard time catching on to them—until they encounter a first-rate production, which renders all the alleged musical difficulty moot. Let me explain.

There is no intrinsic reason why anyone should walk

out of *Wozzeck* or Arnold Schoenberg's *Erwartung* or any of the other avant-garde operas of the expressionist period. No reason, that is, except ignorance. Believe it or not, the boogeyman *Wozzeck* originally was a hit. The opera was a succès de scandale at its premiere in Berlin and quickly entered the repertoires of opera houses all over Austria and Germany; it was even given its American premiere, in Philadelphia, in 1931. What dented *Wozzeck*'s rise was not its idiom but its politics; the Nazis trashed it as an example of "decadent music" and, bereft of its huge performance base in central Europe, it stood outside the standard repertoire by the time sanity, and the Allies, prevailed.

In other words, had music been allowed to taken its natural course, we would easily see that *Wozzeck,* brilliantly original though it is, stands squarely in the same *Mitteleuropäisch* mainstream that we otherwise find so appealing. The postwar conservatism that engulfed the American musical scene didn't help matters. In fact, the musical history of the twentieth century, in a nutshell, is that public tastes never quite caught up with what composers were doing, thanks in part to the extreme dislocation of the war years.

Luckily, the past decade has seen a demystification of modern opera, and today not even small children are frightened of it. Works like Béla Bartók's *Duke Bluebeard's Castle,* Stravinsky's *The Rake's Progress,* and Benjamin Britten's *Peter Grimes* and *Death in Venice* seem positively stodgy. I remain utterly resistant to the putative charms of Sir Michael Tippett's quirky operas, such as *The Midsummer Marriage,* but find the music of his German contemporary Hans Werner Henze (*Elegy for Young Lovers, We Come to the River*) both arresting and compelling. But the real action today comes from the pens of younger composers such as John Adams, whose *Nixon in China* was a dazzling first foray into opera, William Bolcom (the eclectic *McTeague*) and, in Britain, Harrison Birtwistle

(*Gawain*). And, of course, Philip Glass, the man whose reputation among those who loathe him has gone directly from far-out radical to old-hat conservative. The fecund Glass, however, is the author of at least two indubitable masterpieces, *Einstein on the Beach* and *Satyagraha* and may be busy writing another right now, for all we know.

Back in his fire-breathing days, the composer and conductor Pierre Boulez opined that we should blow up all the opera houses, since they were useless anachronisms. A couple of years ago, I witnessed one of the most stirring operatic performances of my life, a production of Debussy's *Pelléas et Mélisande* in Paris. The conductor was . . . Pierre Boulez.

So maybe there's life in the old grande dame yet. As this brief survey shows, the form of opera has changed and mutated over the centuries, lurching from lavish spectacle to dark psychological drama and back again. It has been denounced as a frivolous and expensive plaything of the idle rich and praised as the most democratic of all the arts.

Certainly, in our day opera has staged an impressive comeback. Since Glass and his librettist Robert Wilson took New York by storm with *Einstein* in 1976, the best and brightest musical minds have headed for the opera house. It's the best place for them to be—and for us as well.

Chapter 4

Prima la musica e poi le parole, or Is It the Other Way Around?

For music any words are good enough.

—ARISTOPHANES, *THE BIRDS*

Where words leave off, music begins.

—HEINRICH HEINE

If music could be translated into human speech, it would no longer need to exist.

—NED ROREM

Practically from the beginning of opera, composers and audiences have been arguing over which ought to come first, the words or the music. Today, that may seem a silly question to which the answer is self-evident, but it wasn't always so. The theoreticians of the Middle Ages posited a division between poetry and music; poetry, according to one, was "musique naturelle," while song was "musique artificielle." At several points in operatic history, pitched battles have raged over the issue, and at least twice a major reformer has come along to set things straight.

First it was Christoph Willibald Gluck, who together with his influential librettist Raniero de' Calzabigi came down on the side of the text during a time of widespread musical abuses, largely perpetrated by show-off singers: "I sought to restrict music to its true purpose of expressing the poetry and reinforcing the dramatic situation, without interrupting the action or hampering it with superfluous embellishments," he wrote, and certainly his heart was in the right place. For opera in the late eighteenth century was rife with what we would today call abuses—ever-fancier arias written on demand for singers, interpolated notes and runs not in the score, etc.—and Gluck was seeking to strip it down, returning to the impulse that had created it in the first place.

The second great reformer was Richard Wagner, who was not only one of the most influential figures in musical history but in Western cultural history in general. Wagner not only *re*formed opera, he *trans*formed it, and arrogantly (the only way he knew how to do anything) "preempted to himself the very concept of opera," as the eminent musicologist Joseph Kerman wrote in his seminal study, *Opera as Drama.*

This whole discussion of words versus music really takes us back to some of the discussion in chapter one. What is opera? Why does it have the hold on our imaginations that it does? How does it manage its effects? And how can we learn to heighten our appreciation of it? Sure, you can listen to Pavarotti's "Nessun dorma" until the neighbors call the cops, and you can enjoy it on a simple, tuneful level. But, believe me, it's far more rewarding to understand Calaf's Act III aria from *Turandot* in context, if only for the reason that then you might actually want to get to know the whole opera, instead of just three minutes of it.

So what is the essence of opera? What are those qualities that distinguish it from all other art forms and elevate it above them all? What has attracted to it all manner of talented mortals—not only those who made their living as composers but great authors (Thomas Mann comes immediately to mind, and Anthony Burgess), philosophers (Voltaire, who wrote many librettos for Jean-Philippe Rameau), and filmmakers (Coppola, Scorsese), whose works are either frankly operatic or contain elements of opera in them? (Who can forget Coppola's staging of Mascagni's *Cavalleria rusticana* as the finale of his *Godfather* epic, or Scorsese's use of the same opera's famous Intermezzo to accompany Robert De Niro's pugilistic exploits in *Raging Bull*? What is its most important element: the music or the words?)

Or maybe even something else? Jean-Jacques Rousseau, in addition to being one of the eighteenth century's most influential philosophers and worst human beings (see Paul Johnson's *Intellectuals* for the gory details), was also a composer and theorist who wrote several operas and contributed articles on music to Diderot's great *Encyclopédie,* which he later collected as his *Dictionnaire de musique* in 1768. Rousseau defined opera as "a dramatic and lyrical spectacle in which one endeavors to combine all the graces of the fine arts in the representation of a passionate action, with the intention of arousing interest and creating illusion by means of pleasant sensations. The constituent parts are the libretto, the music and the scenery. . . ."

Wait just a minute, Jean-Jacques; the scenery? Well, yes. In the eighteenth century, spectacle was as much a part of the very notion of opera as it is of the Broadway/West End musical. When operas were planned, very often the last and least of the considerations was who was actually going to compose the damn thing. Far higher on the production food chain were the text, the casting of the singers, and the splendor of the sets. The composer, tagging along at the end, was expected to tailor his score to the capabilities of the singers and the resources of the theater, not the other way around. The very notion of a composer presenting a score for production, and refusing to alter a single note as if the very music were the blueprint of the entire event, would have been laughable. Imagine if, say, a famous contemporary musical got the same treatment:

TREVOR NUNN AND JOHN NAPIER
present
T. S. Eliot's
CATS
starring
ELAINE PAIGE as GRIZABELLA
music by a. l. webber

Hard to imagine, isn't it? And yet, even during Mozart's prime, that was the way it was. Mozart's operas exist in variant versions, according to the location of the performance and the lineup of singers he had to work with. One of the great mysteries of opera is why *Don Giovanni,* one of Mozart's masterpieces and certainly a strong candidate for the mythical title of Greatest Opera Ever Written, contains no real arias for the title character: "Fin ch'han dal vino," the so-called champagne aria, is over in a flash (the singer draws only one breath during its course). Mozart was taking a lemon (the limitations of the twenty-one-year-old Luigi Bassi, who created the role) and making lemonade. It is not until the end of *Don Giovanni* that the legendary rakehell is revealed as the tragic hero he is, standing up to the devil with head unbowed and being dragged down to perdition for his integrity. Why bother to have the Don explain himself when we get an even more rounded portrait from the other major characters (the three women, his trusty manservant), each of whom sees him in a different way?

Just how ironclad the importance of venue was in the eighteenth century may be inferred from remarks in a 1725 letter written by Giuseppe Riva, a representative at the English court, concerning the operas of George Frideric Handel, the German-born composer whose career in England was heavily occupied with Italian opera. To Riva, who hailed from Modena, "the operas that are given in England, however fine as music, are nevertheless ruined by their poetry. In England people like very few recitatives, thirty airs, and at least one duet, distributed over the three acts. The subject must be simple, tender, heroic—Roman, Greek or possibly Persian, but never Gothic or Lombard. For this year and for the next two years there must be two equal parts for Cuzzoni and Faustina [two famous leading ladies of the day]. Senesino [a castrato, or surgically altered male soprano] takes the principal male characters, and his part must be heroic. . . . If the subject demands three women, a third woman may be employed, as there is a third singer here to take part." In other words, there were plenty of prima donnas, tapping their toes and waiting for parts written to order.

My point is that the very notion of what constitutes opera is constantly in flux, which is the way it should be. Every age gets the kind of opera it wants—or maybe deserves. Through history, opera has reflected the society into which it was born, from the Greek-obssessed poesy of the courts of seventeenth-century Italy to the protocol- and position-conscious arias sung in the royal châteaux of eighteenth-century France and Austria, to the politically dominated choruses of nineteenth-century revolutionary Europe to the alienated, semipsychoanalytic interior monologues of our own time. Like the novel or the play, the opera is a mirror of the times and conditions prevailing at its birth, and the greatest operas offer a direct, emotional insight into the past.

By the time we get to Mozart, it's clear that while performance conditions still count very heavily in the composer's overall conception, a new, more independent streak of thought is beginning to creep in. Here is Mozart writing to his formidable Da, detailing the circumstances of *The Abduction from the Seraglio.* In a letter dated September 26, 1781, Mozart first comments on the ways he has modified Gottlieb Stephanie's libretto:

"As the original text began with a monologue, I asked Herr Stephanie to make a little arietta out of it, and then to put in a duet instead of making the two chatter together after Osmin's short song. As we have given the part of Osmin [the comic harem overseer] to Herr Fischer, who certainly has an excellent bass voice . . . we must take advantage of it, particularly as he has the whole Viennese public on his side. I have explained to Stephanie the words I require for [Osmin's] aria—indeed I had finished composing most of the music for it before Stephanie knew anything whatever about it."

Mozart, in other words, is already starting to alter the balance of power. A couple of weeks later, he writes to his father once more, and this time his attitude is quite clear:

"I am well aware that the verse is not of the best, but it fitted in and it agreed so well with the musical ideas that were already buzzing in my head that it could not fail to please me. . . . Besides, I should say that in an opera *the poetry must be altogether the obedient daughter of the music.* Why do Italian comic operas find favor everywhere, in spite of the miserable libretti? Because there the music reigns supreme, and when one listens to it all else is forgotten. . . . The best thing of all is when a good composer, who understands the stage and is talented enough to make sound suggestions, meets an able poet, that true phoenix; in that case no fears need be entertained as to the applause even of the ignorant."

Mozart was not suggesting that the libretto was unimportant; he reserves most of his complaints in these letters to texts that (in his view) were needlessly concerned with rhyming for the sake of rhyming, prizing form over function; like playground basketball players, librettists of the day were more concerned with looking good than actually being good. "If we composers were always to stick so faithfully to our rules," noted Mozart, "we should be concocting music as unpalatable as their libretti."

Before anyone else, Mozart understood (why? how?) that in opera words and music formed a partnership, but that the music must needs take precedence when push came to shove. Mozart therefore is rightly regarded as opera's first great composer-dramatist, and though he wrote his best operas on texts by an extremely able librettist, Lorenzo Da Ponte (whose stature is such that people still honor his name), he was never in doubt that it was the music that was the engine of the opera, and nothing else.

The words, however, exist to supply the dramatic context that fires the composer's imagination. I've already discussed the Letter Scene in Tchaikovsky's *Eugene Onegin,* which happens to be the very first bit of the opera the composer set to music. Tatiana's passionate outburst of repressed love found a sympathetic breast in Tchaikovsky's (the composer's own necessarily repressed homosexuality tormented him all his life), and it is little wonder that the letter scene was the first thing he put to pen. But what if the words, instead of expressing a young girl's first, mad love, were merely Tatiana's to-do list:

1. Wake up
2. Have breakfast
3. Beat serfs
4. Lunch w/Olga
5. Flirt w/handsome stranger
6. Dinner w/Mama and Papa
7. Attend proto-Bolshevik rally (and be sure to wear something red!)
8. Bedtime

The music would likely have been very different indeed.

It is said of some composers that they could set the telephone book to music—in *Der Rosenkavalier,* Richard Strauss actually did set a stage direction in Hugo von Hofmannsthal's libretto. The British composer Michael Tippett writes his own librettos, and perhaps a phone book would make more sense. But most composers need the stimulus of dramatic words and deeds to get the juices flowing, and if the best opera librettos are not likely to win any literary prizes (and, with the exception of those by Da Ponte and Hofmannsthal, they generally won't), they do provide the launching pad for music's highest flights of the imagination.

And while it is true that a great libretto does not necessarily ensure a great opera, it is equally true that a hopeless libretto will pretty much mean an opera's downfall. Franz Schubert, a wonderful songwriter, tried his hand at opera many times but was always defeated by a lack of a decent libretto. Schubert has been dead since 1828, so the issue is moot, but the question remains open whether, had he had a libretto worthy of his talents, he could have written a great opera. Surely he could have done better than *The Devil's Pleasure Palace, Alfonso and Estrella,* and *Fierrabras?*

Maybe not. Not every composer has the ability or the temperament to work successfully in opera. Beethoven, after several stabs at it, wrote only one, the flawed masterpiece *Fidelio.* The other two Bs, Bach and Brahms, wrote none. Gustav Mahler, a great symphonic and song-cycle composer, one of the greatest conductors in history, and the leader of both the Vienna Opera and the Metropolitan Opera, never tried his hand at opera, except to complete and edit Carl Maria von Weber's lesser effort, *Die drei Pintos.* To write an opera demands a range of skills that are not limited simply to the musical. The opera composer must also be a judge of literary merit, able to work collegially if not congenially with a partner; a student of the theater, knowing exactly which effects are possible on stage; and an impresario, adept in the ways of money-raising and patronage.

The nineteenth century, which was dominated by the twin giants Giuseppe Verdi and Richard Wagner, also witnessed the triumph of the music over words. Curiously, though, words were of paramount importance to both Verdi and Wagner. Verdi, who was a very active collaborator, repeatedly got into trouble with the censors of his time over the often politically incendiary subject matter of his operas; both *Rigoletto* and *Un ballo in maschera* had to have their locations changed, since the assassination of a ruling monarch was not exactly a theme designed to find favor in whichever principality the opera was being premiered. And let's not forget that, for his last two (and two greatest) operas, Verdi turned to none other than Shakespeare, whose plays *Othello* and *The Merry Wives of Windsor* form the bases for the operas *Otello* and *Falstaff;* the librettist for both was a fellow composer, Arrigo Boito, another great wordsmith whose literary contributions to opera have kept his name alive.

Wagner, on the other hand, wrote his own texts. (He did not call them operas, and he hated the term *libretto.*) The composer himself prized his texts very highly, often entertaining, if that is the correct word, his guests with dramatic readings while he was at work on the music. (He wrote the poems first.) In his great *Ring of the Nibelung* cycle of four music dramas, Wagner went so far as to invent a whole new dialect of German, a kind of personal *Ur-Deutsch* in which he couched his characters' motivations. Wagner also was a producer par excellence, who inveigled various crowned heads to give him money, finally erecting his own monument in the form of the Festspielhaus in Bayreuth (say "BUY-roit," not Beirut), Germany, where the first performance of the *Ring* was given in 1876. (To illustrate the unity of operatic history, the *Ring* was initially conceived as a festival piece along the lines of the celebration of Dionysus at Athens.)

The determination of even as great a melodist as Verdi to get the words right may be gleaned from the technical detail in a letter Boito wrote to him in 1881 concerning *Otello.* In the Verdi-Boito collaboration, nothing was left to chance; both men were conscious not only of serving Shakespeare well, but of creating something that, in many ways, would be an improvement on the sainted original:

> *The ensemble has, as we planned, its lyrical and its dramatic parts fused together. That is to say, we have a lyrical and melodic piece superimposed upon a dramatic dialogue. The principal character of the lyrical part is Desdemona; that of the dramatic part is Iago. Thus Iago, having been stunned for a moment by an event beyond his control . . . suddenly takes up all the threads of the tragedy with unequaled speed and energy, making the catastrophe his and using the unforeseen event to hasten the course of the final disaster. All this was in Shakespeare's mind and is clearly expressed in our work.*

Boito then moves on to a little shop talk:

> *We had agreed that the lyrical portion of the ensemble should have one meter and the dialogue portion (the chorus included) another. This I have arranged. The*

> *meter of the dialogue is endecasyllabic. You can break it up at your convenience; broken up, it resolves itself naturally into five-stress lines. You can employ both meters at your discretion. The device was called for because endecasyllabics, sustained throughout a lyrical movement, would appear too somber, and five-stress lines too frivolous. I did not want to mix the two meters visibly but have preferred the artifice just now explained to you. I am fully convinced it will produce the desired effect.*

Whew! Pretty complicated stuff. But you don't have to be an endecasyllabic scientist to realize that there is a lot more that goes into the creation of a singable, dramatic opera libretto than just picking up a play and slapping some music to it—although, in *Wozzeck,* Alban Berg did basically just that with Büchner's play and in so doing created the greatest of all twentieth-century operas. The exception that proves the rule, as it were.

The composer-librettist correspondence of the nineteenth and early twentieth centuries makes fascinating reading today, and not just because the telephone has replaced the letter as the preferred medium of informational exchange. Whether the two colleagues were fast friends (not very often) or pitched enemies (more often than you might think), both parties to an operatic transaction were determined to get the technical details exactly right. As proud as Boito might have been about his own contributions, though, the sense of his letter cited above makes it clear that his words are meant to serve the composer, who, in turn, is serving the dramatic situation.

Which, in the end, is what opera is all about. Professor Kerman had it right when he titled his influential book *Opera as Drama.* The title was a reference to Wagner's 1851 essay "*Oper und Drama,*" in which Wagner articulated his goal of a completely unified work of art—the *Gesamtkunstwerk*—in which poetic, musical, and scenic elements would be welded together. "The unified artistic form," wrote Wagner in his turgid, pseudo-Hegelian prose, "can only be conceived as a manifestation of a unified content. A unified content can only be recognized by its being given an artistic expression that directly communicates with our feelings. A content that makes a twofold expression necessary—an expression, that is, which forces the author to turn alternately to reason and feeling—must likewise be divided and ambiguous."

Got that?

Wagner went on to lay out his beef against traditional opera.

> *Up to now, the composer did not even try to achieve unity of form for his entire work, each single number having its independently filled-out form and being related to the other closed numbers of the opera only in point of external structure, but possessing no actual affinity based on subject matter. Incoherence was thus peculiar to operatic music. . . . In summarizing, we designate as the most perfect unified form of art that in which the widest range of human experiences is conveyed to the feelings in so completely intelligible a manner that the manifestation of this content at every point of the action first arouses and then satisfies the emotions.*

So don't worry if you can't follow Boito's nattering about meter or Wagner's Teutonic hair-splitting. The point is that, in creating their operas, the greatest composers have always sought to avoid answering the question posed by the title of this chapter. They may have thought that, like Gluck, they were serving the word by enabling the text to be projected clearly and intelligibly by the singers. Or they may have believed, as Verdi and Wagner did, that the real work of art lay in wedding the two together.

In the end, though, whether consciously or not, they all subscribed to Mozart's famous dictum about poetry being the obedient daughter of music. Gluck's *Orfeo, Iphigénie en Aulide,* and *Iphigénie en Tauride* live on today not on the strength of their texts but by the power and beauty of Gluck's melodies. Verdi, in tackling Shakespeare, was sure setting himself up for, if not an invidious comparison, then certainly a fall. And yet the majesty of his music transforms his source into something even greater than Shakespeare himself could have imagined. And Wagner, for all his pride of authorship of the *Ring*'s poem, knew the text could never be understood until the entire cycle, in all its incredible glory, could be properly staged, in a theater he designed himself at Bayreuth.

My recommendation, therefore, is that you as a budding opera fan familiarize yourself with the libretto before buying a ticket to the Met or to your local opera house; that you read the text carefully, with a good synopsis at hand to help you sort out the various Marquis de This from the Barons de That (any decent recording will contain libretto, translations, and synopses, along with detailed program notes). Because without a grounding in the locale, action, and historical background of the opera, the tunes may register in your mind and on your tongue but they will lack the deeper level of meaning with which composer and librettist have spent so much time investing them.

Sure, it takes time. Sure, it smacks of study hall. Sure, trying to follow along in Italian, German, and Russian ain't easy for those of us who never got past Mr. Cheswell's first-year French course. But nobody ever said this opera stuff was going to be painless.

And once you're past the basics—the who, what, where, when, why, and how of the setting—you're free to sit back, relax, and let the fabulous music wash over you, secure in the knowledge that while the other guy may think "Nessun dorma" is something they sing at a soccer match in Italy, you know what it's really all about. That's when the real fun begins.

And, of course, the real work.

Chapter 5

A (Not Quite) Totally Arbitrary Basic Repertoire, or Do I Have to Listen to *All* of Them?

Of all the affected, sapless, soulless, beginningless, endless, topless, bottomless, topsiturviest, scrannel-pipiest, tongs and boniest doggerel of sounds I ever endured the deadliest of, that eternity of nothing was the deadliest.

—JOHN RUSKIN, ON *DIE MEISTERSINGER*

We went to Mannheim and attended a shivaree—otherwise an opera—the one called Lohengrin. *The banging and slamming and booming and crashing were something beyond belief.*

—MARK TWAIN, *A TRAMP ABROAD*

If an opera cannot be played by an organ-grinder, then that opera is not going to achieve immortality.

—SIR THOMAS BEECHAM

I suppose this is the part you've been waiting for. I am looking forward to telling you all about my favorite operas, why they're my favorites, and why I think they are likely to become your favorites too. (Not your only favorites, of course.) And we'll get right to the honor roll in just a minute. But first, a word on the selections.

Let me state my prejudices right up front. I have two of them. As mentioned, I do not much care for the bel canto operas of Bellini, Donizetti, and Rossini; in fact, I find them nearly impossible to sit through, for reasons already explained. Neither am I a big fan of baroque opera as exemplified by Handel, although I understand and respect the enthusiasm of its admirers. On the other hand, I utterly reject as ignorant and crabbed of soul the fashionable disparagement of Puccini as a cheap sensationmonger.

Other than that, I am a model of open-mindedness. When people ask me which is my favorite opera (or, worse, my preferred composer), I am hard pressed to answer, as any right-thinking individual of catholic and sophisticated taste should be. The reason is that I don't have one. I am an impartial arbiter, wholly lacking in any particular ideology or political agenda. Although my list is comprehensive, it is by no means deliberately inclusive; there are no operas by Aleutian Islanders, Eskimos, Filipinos, Arabs, or Native Americans. There are, on the other hand, works by Germans, Austrians, Italians, Frenchmen, Czechs, Russians, and Americans, both white and black; there are operas written by straights and gays, Jews and goys; there are operas written by both the quick and the dead. There is, however, not a single opera by a woman, for the simple reason that none has yet made its way into the repertoire. (Sorry, ladies.)

As you cruise the list, you will encounter some familiar standard works from all periods of operatic history and a couple of oddball choices written within living memory. The dreaded twelve-tone system will raise its ugly head, as will the controversial minimalist school. There are operas based on Pushkin and Goethe, and there is an opera based on an episode in the life of Richard and Pat Nixon; there are operas sung in the usual foreign languages, as well as in plain English, of both the British and the American varieties, and there is even one sung in Sanskrit. Historical personages such as Saint Francis make an appearance, as do Henry Kissinger, a Russian czar, Don Juan, and the Mahatma Gandhi. Some of the operas take place in palaces, others in prison camps. Some of the characters have sexual intercourse with each other, usually illicitly; some get pregnant; some commit incest; some are pederasts and rapists; some are murderers. A few die of deadly infectious diseases; others commit suicide by shooting themselves or jumping into rivers. One even pulls down the entire universe around her shoulders. All, however, are human—all too human.

Which is, as I've noted, the essential condition for opera—that it be about real people (no matter how extravagant or exotic their predilections), and that it have something to say to us about the way we live our lives, and the social and moral circumstances in which we find ourselves.

You won't find much in the way of plot summaries here. Nothing is more boring than a précis of an opera you don't know and perhaps never heard of. Instead, what I've tried to do is to lead you into the opera by discussing its place in history, as well as salient aspects of its composition and the techniques the composer has used in constructing it—how it fits in, in other words, with the issues

I've raised in this book. In this way, I hope you'll find the operas interesting to read about both before you listen to them and again after you get to know them. In fact, I hope you do come back to the book after you've become an expert on, say, *Così fan tutte* or *Wozzeck,* to argue with me or to add your own observations to my brilliant analyses.

And so, without further ado, and in the order it pleases me to present them for your consideration (yes, there is an internal logic at work here, as you will notice eventually), here they are: The Basic Opera Repertoire for the Waning Days (thank God) of the Twentieth Century.

Béla Bartók: *Duke Bluebeard's Castle* (*A kékszakállú herceg vára*). Dark, dark, dark. Gloomy, even. Depressing. A two-hander. And sung in Hungarian to boot. Not your basic *Barber of Seville* laugh riot. So why is this opera listed first?

A number of reasons, most of them for your own good. It's a twentieth-century work, composed in 1911 and first performed in Budapest in 1918. It's short (less than an hour in duration, which makes it easy to absorb but difficult to program—what do you do for a second act?). It's written in a "modern" but eminently approachable tonal idiom that should pose no problems for a listener of even modest sophistication. It is a near-perfect marriage of text and music by two of turn-of-the-century Hungary's most adventurous artists. And yet, it's a deep, dense, challenging work that plumbs the psyches of two archetypal characters, and one that will keep you up nights thinking about what it means. In short, it's a ideal example of all the issues we've been discussing up to now.

The opera begins with a spoken prologue, which is almost always omitted in performance (except in Hungary, of course). One of its stanzas says explicitly:

Enter! A realm awaits you that without you
Cannot come into being; the realm of myth!
Still thinking of your lives? Find them here with

New meanings, for our story is about you,
Ladies and gentlemen.

In other words, what we are about to see is not the fairy tale of Bluebeard and his nosy wives—or rather, not simply that story, but something more. True, the "plot" conforms to the familiar tale: Bluebeard takes a new wife, Judith, and brings her home to his drafty, sepulchral castle. At first, the place seems pretty grim, but as Bluebeard gradually unlocks the secrets of his fortress, it becomes ever grander until, at the fifth door, his entire kingdom is revealed. But Judith, being Woman, wants more. (What *do* women want?) The sixth door exposes a vast lake, watered by tears, while behind the seventh lie imprisoned Bluebeard's three previous wives. Now Judith must join them; the door shuts and Bluebeard is alone once more, this time forever.

Not exactly a bedroom farce, eh? Well, it's not supposed to be. Instead Bartók and Béla Balázs, the librettist, are attempting nothing less than the exploration of the human soul. The opera begins in blackest night; as the various doors—revealing the torture chamber, the armory, the treasury, the garden—open, each one streaked with blood, the dismal castle grows brighter until the climactic opening of the fifth door (in a resplendent blaze of C major). Each of the five rooms conducts us a step further into Bluebeard's heart, but not even the magnificence of the fifth door is immune from the "blood motive" in the music, a minor second—play any two adjacent black and white notes on the piano simultaneously to see what I mean. Bluebeard's agony is always close to the surface, and when Judith pushes him beyond the point he cares to go, she finds only the Lake of Sorrow and, in the end, the same imprisoned fate his other wives found earlier. The last scene in the opera belongs to Bluebeard, who sings passionately about each of his loves, who represent the morning, noon, and evening of his life. Now Judith, the night, and the most beautiful of all, has to take her place with them, and Bluebeard must remain, alone, in the endless darkness of solitude.

Bluebeard's Castle is not only a splendid example of twentieth-century opera, it can stand for all opera in its melodic urgency, its subtle, penetrating harmonies, the efficiency of its construction, the melding of its words and music (*Warning:* Do not try to translate this opera into English or any other language, or its warranty immediately expires), and, most of all, the sheer beauty of its music. Bartók was just beginning his pioneering researches into the wellsprings of Hungarian folk music, which were to have such a large effect on his subsequent compositional style, and the first fruits of this labor are evident in *Bluebeard.* Also audible is the composer's fascination with Debussy, whose opera *Pelléas et Mélisande* dates from 1902.

The composer never wrote another work like *Bluebeard's Castle* (indeed, he never wrote another opera, and more's the pity); his other stage works—*The Wooden Prince* and *The Miraculous Mandarin*—are ballets. No doubt the enormous obstacles placed in his opera's way—Bartók entered it in a Budapest competition, but the jury rejected it as unperformable—had much to do with his reluctance to continue with the genre. But Bartók said all he had to say in *Bluebeard's Castle,* and said it in the unmistakable accents of genius.

Jacques Offenbach: *The Tales of Hoffmann (Les contes d'Hoffmann).* Stella! You never know where the next masterpiece is going to come from. And who would expect it to be from the pen of a composer best known for his frothy comic operas, the can-do author of the can-can, and the man who put the oo-la-la in the Second Empire? But, then, almost nothing about Offenbach is what one might have expected. A German Jew, the second son of a cantor whose surname originally had been Eberst (Offenbach is the name of a town outside Frankfurt), young

Jakob was a cello prodigy whose skill got him shipped off to Paris, where he eventually found his way into the cello section of the Opéra-Comique.

Offenbach's reputation in his own time was almost entirely as a composer of comic operas and operettas, such as *Orpheus in the Underworld,* the first full-length operetta ever written, *La belle Hélène, Barbe-bleue* (that pesky Bluebeard again), *La vie parisienne, The Grand Duchess of Gerolstein* and *La Périchole.* Who, then, would have thought that his masterpiece would have been *The Tales of Hoffmann,* a sprawling five-act opera that is as tuneful as anything Offenbach ever wrote, but which is far from comique?

The plot, based on various fantastic and grotesque stories by the German romantic writer E. T. A. Hoffmann, is picaresque. Hoffmann, a poet, describes his three lost loves—Olympia, who turns out to be a mechanical doll; Antonia, an intense young woman who literally sings herself to death before Hoffmann's eyes; and Giulietta, a faithless Venetian courtesan. The action is framed by two acts (or a prologue and an epilogue) in which we see Hoffmann and his companion, Nicklausse, in a tavern, musing on Hoffmann's real love, an opera singer named Stella. Every step of the way, his footsteps are dogged by various incarnations of his rival for Stella's hand, the councillor Lindorf. Operatic tradition dictates that the same bass-baritone take the roles of Lindorf, Coppélius, Dr. Miracle, and Dapertutto; less often, the three heroines are sung by the same soprano.

There are some operas that, for various reasons, have never achieved a final form. *Boris Godunov* is, famously, one such; *Hoffmann* is another. That is to say, no one can quite agree on what the composer meant the work's ultimate shape and content to be. Bits and pieces of the opera were intended at first for other works, and then dragooned: the famous Barcarolle originally was composed for an ill-fated serious opera, *Die Rheinnixen* (*The Rhinemaidens*). In the case of *Hoffmann,* the arguments concern not only the ordering of the acts but the ending as well, since Offenbach passed away before completing much of the fourth (Venetian) act, and the end of the fifth; additionally, the orchestration was left unbegun.

When Offenbach died in 1880 during rehearsals (in order to support his family, he had also been frantically composing other operettas at the same time), the composer Ernest Guiraud took *Hoffmann* under his wing. Guiraud dropped the Venetian act and shortened the mezzo-soprano role of Nicklausse because the singer wasn't up to the demands of the part; thus began the "tradition" of doing pretty much anything to poor *Hoffmann.* Mahler, for example, chucked the first and fifth acts, which depict Hoffmann drowning his sorrows over his love for Stella in Luther's tavern in Nuremberg. In 1977 the musicologist Fritz Oeser published a critical edition that, most likely, is the closest approximation to the composer's intentions we're ever going to have.

It doesn't matter. *Hoffmann* is a masterpiece just about any way you care to perform it. And thus we come to a conundrum that was best articulated by Jonathan Miller in his book *Subsequent Performances.* Discussing what he calls a work's "afterlife," Miller argues that we would not, for example, prize the Belvedere torso so highly if the figure had its head, arms, and legs restored; likewise, the Venus de Milo. We have transformed those sculptures into works of art, "creating" a new entity unimagined and unintended by its author. The work of art thus exists at least partly in the eye of the beholder.

So—so what if the Venetian act (often known as the Giulietta act after the name of its heroine) comes before or after the Antonia act? Or whether the Barcarolle was written for a failed opera? Or whether *Hoffmann* is performed with spoken dialogue or recitatives (a problem that also plagues another great unfinished French masterpiece, *Carmen,* as we shall see)? What we treasure about *Hoffmann* is not only the great melodic set pieces, such as

Olympia's birdsong and Dapertutto's "Diamond" aria, but the opera's overall air of romantic menace and mystery.

And its ending. Part of *Hoffmann's* afterlife is its quintessentially bleak conclusion. After regaling the students in Luther's tavern with his hard-luck tales, and winning their sympathy, Hoffmann is too drunk to care when Stella leaves on Lindorf's arm. The Muse of Poetry claims Hoffmann for herself; suffering, she says, will make him a greater poet. But will it? Or is the whole tale merely the self-justifying delusion of a talentless drunkard—a hack who imagines himself an artist? It seems a particularly apposite lesson for our century.

Modest Mussorgsky: *Boris Godunov.* Speaking of the afterlife, there is no better illustration of its power than *Boris Godunov,* by common consent the greatest of all Russian operas and one of the towering artistic masterpieces in any genre. And speaking of drunkards, Mussorgsky was a heroic one who drank himself into an early grave and left us with a mess—not only in *Boris* but in other works as well.

The story concerns the late sixteenth-century usurpation of the throne by Czar Boris, who (in this version) has murdered the legitimate successor, the young boy Dmitri. Boris, however, is haunted by his deed and when a "false Dmitri" arises in the hinterlands, and eventually raises the Polish army to march on Mother Russia, he is stricken by his conscience. In one of opera's most magisterial scenes, Boris collapses on the throne and dies as the country goes to hell in a handbasket.

That's about all that happens. What makes *Boris* so great, however, is its pitiless examination of the character of each of its principals: the driven (but sympathetic) Boris; the scheming Dmitri; the ambitious Polish princess Marina; the slippery adviser Prince Shuisky. Last but not least is the character of the People, as represented by the chorus, which in this opera assumes an importance hitherto unprecedented in operatic history. From the very first scene, where the suffering Russian masses comment cynically on the machinations going on behind the walls of the Novodevichy monastery and the Kremlin, the chorus is very much a key player in everything that follows.

(This innovative use of the chorus set a pattern for later Russian opera—and also, oddly, for American opera. Because the opera that most closely resembles *Boris* is, of all things, George Gershwin's *Porgy and Bess.* Gershwin's father was from Russia, and *Porgy* is essentially a Russian opera in blackface.)

Bartók's problems in getting *Bluebeard's Castle* produced were nothing compared with what Mussorgsky had to go through. And this accounts, in large part, for the many different versions in which *Boris* exists. The first version began when the composer abruptly abandoned his work on what otherwise would have been his first opera, a setting of Gogol's comedy *The Marriage,* and took up Pushkin's historical drama. (Where would Russian opera be without Pushkin?) He worked at fever pitch, fashioning the libretto himself and starting the music in October of 1868; it was finished the following July and the orchestration was complete by December. Brilliant it was, but the opera was nevertheless rejected by the Maryinsky Theater for a variety of reasons, both practical and political.

Chief among the practical reasons was that the opera lacked any love interest, or indeed any lead female role. So, in Version II, completed in 1872, Mussorgsky composed an entirely new third act (the Polish act), in which Princess Marina appears prominently. He also threw out a scene near the opera's end, set in front of the famous Saint Basil's Cathedral just outside the Kremlin, in which the troubled Czar Boris confronts his disaffected populace and encounters the Simpleton, who predicts a grim future for the Motherland. (Anyone who has ever spent any time in Russia knows this prediction is always safe.) He replaced it with the Kromy Forest scene, in which the people embrace the false Dmitri and the Simpleton is left alone to lament the fate of his country. And he revised the remainder of the opera pretty thoroughly, adding here and cutting there, enriching everywhere. The first performance was a success, largely due to the efforts of Julia Platonova, the first Marina, who demanded that it be staged as a benefit for her. The public loved it, but critics hated it, and by 1882, *Boris* had been dropped from the repertoire.

Enter Nicolai Rimsky-Korsakov, who in 1896 (Mussorgsky had died in 1881) revised and completely rescored the piece, making some cuts and composing some new material to fill in the gaps. The Rimsky version was adopted by the great Russian bass Fyodor Chaliapin, who became identified with the title role. Still unsatisfied, Rimsky made a second performing version, in which he restored the cuts but kept his own additions, and it is this edition that most of us know today. In 1940, Shostakovich made his own edition, which reached back to Mussorgsky's first version for its inspiration.

Which is preferable? The answer is: all of them. Because the ideal version of *Boris* is really None of the Above; it ought to comprise *both* the St. Basil's Cathedral scene and the Kromy Forest scene. It ought to have the splendor of Rimsky's admittedly superior command of orchestration instead of Mussorgsky's dour little noodlings. It ought to have the stark power of Mussorgsky's first, brutal version instead of the prettifications of the Polish act. It ought to have the lyric beauty of the Polish act instead of the relentless gloom of Version I. It ought to have, in short, everything.

Lately, the trend has been to stage one of the two Mussorgsky versions (real purists eschew the Polish act altogether), but the Rimsky incarnation has achieved a legitimacy in its own right. My advice to the novice is to get to know the Rimsky version, then dig deeper into the composer's original thoughts. Either way, you can't go wrong. And before long, you'll be a Pushkin fan, too.

If *Boris* appeals, you might want to investigate some other Russian operas from the same period: Mussorgsky's *Khovanshchina* and, perhaps more approachable, Alexander Borodin's *Prince Igor,* another opera left incomplete at the composer's death and finished by the ubiquitous Rimsky-Korsakov (with help from another prominent Russian composer, Alexander Glazunov, who reconstructed the overture from his memory after hearing Borodin play it on the piano—yeah, right). One excerpt from *Prince Igor* you might already know are the Polovtsian Dances; if you don't know them, you certainly know some of the pop tunes that have been fashioned from them, such as "Stranger in Paradise."

John Adams: *Nixon in China* and *The Death of Klinghoffer.* Operas about historical personages are nothing new. (See above.) What is new are operas about real people who were still walking among us at the time of the opera's composition. Such a work is John Adams's groundbreaking *Nixon in China,* the first result of a remarkable artistic collaboration among Adams, librettist Alice Goodman, and director Peter Sellars. Based on the late president's epochal 1972 visit to Red China, the opera was premiered in Houston on October 22, 1987 (the same week as the stock market crash)—a mere fifteen years between deed and drama.

Everyone feared the worst. Sellars, the puckish director who had made a name for himself with his radical restagings of various opera and theater classics, was a known firestarter, and Adams was a confessed minimalist; Goodman, for her part, was an American expatriate living in London, which made her loyalties suspect as well. Surely, these three lefties would use the opportunity for a searing indictment of Nixon, one of the least beloved of all American presidents; of his wife, Pat, one of the least beloved of all First Ladies; and Henry Kissinger, one of the least beloved, period.

Well, surprise. What emerged was a finely wrought inner drama of not-quite-great men caught up in great events. Here was Tricky Dick, nervous and insecure, and given a magnificent closing monologue (that is actually part of a larger, complex ensemble). Here is the erstwhile Plastic Pat, trembling like a dewy schoolgirl in her ravishing aria. Here are formidable Maos, Tse-tung and Madam, part icons and part charlatans. Only with Kissinger were the authors unable to resist the temptation to portray the man as a clown and a buffoon.

Nixon in China is filled with dazzling operatic set pieces, beginning with the landing of the Nixons' plane on the tarmac in Peking. The first act ends with a magnificently constructed banquet sequence, while Act II contains a parody performance of the propaganda ballet "The Red Detachment of Women," during which Kissinger becomes so excited that he storms the stage. The final act consists of six intertwined soliloquies, as the principals reflect on the peculiar circumstances of their lives that have led them to this crossroads of history.

Musically, Adams combines his minimalist inclinations with a broader palette that affords him complete command of the drama. There were those in attendance at the premiere who heard nothing but needle-stuck-in-the-groove music (as minimalism was widely described at the time), but sharper ears detected an exciting synthesis of traditional forms with minimalist usage; aside from the idiom, *Nixon* is very much a traditional opera in the same way that, say, Verdi's *Don Carlos* is, and no less remarkable.

The same trio struck again in 1991 with *The Death of Klinghoffer,* once again based on an episode from recent history. This time the subject was the 1985 murder of the wheelchair-bound American Jew Leon Klinghoffer by Palestinian terrorists aboard the hijacked ship *Achille Lauro.* The premiere was in Brussels, but as with *Nixon* the production was shared by a number of international opera houses and the work quickly made its way around the world. *Klinghoffer* is less successful than *Nixon,* and not because of Goodman's guaranteed-to-offend-everyone treatment of the subject matter. (The opera was a signal failure in New York, where some members of the city's large Jewish community were outraged by Goodman's sympathetic treatment of the Palestinians, who were actually represented as human beings.) What *Klinghoffer* lacks is *Nixon*'s high drama; the later work is much closer in spirit to an oratorio than to opera, a feeling emphasized by Sellars's static staging.

Both scores, however, repay home listening. Your chances of encountering *Nixon* or *Klinghoffer* in the opera house, while not exactly nil, are still lower than your chances of catching *Rigoletto.* So buy the CDs, lean back with Goodman's moving librettos, and settle in for two of contemporary music's most satisfying listening experiences. This is not just new music: this is *your* new music, something that will long outlive Nirvana and Pearl Jam (whoever they are—or, by the time you read this, were). So, as the old Trickster might have said: get a mitt and get in the game. You'll be glad you did.

Giuseppi Verdi: *Don Carlos* and *Otello.* Thought I'd never get to an opera you'd heard of, right? Well, wait no longer, because here comes Mean Joe Green himself, the apotheosis of the Italian operatic tradition (in fact, the inventor of much of it), the composer whose works lie snugly at the center of the repertoire, ladies and gentlemen, Giuseppe Verdi.

I am not an unreserved Verdi fan. Too much of his music (and not just the earlier operas), to my ears, is content with organ-grinder accompaniments; too many of his famous melodies content themselves with mediocrity by relying on the most banal sort of sequences. (Think of Count di Luna's "Il balen" from that most ridiculous of Verdi's operas, *Il trovatore.*) In short, too much of early Verdi is too close to Bellini and Donizetti for my money.

Back when I was at the Eastman School of Music, the

eminent musicologist Charles Warren Fox used to tell his students that, with maturity, would come love for Verdi. These words naturally fell upon deaf ears as we know-it-all undergrads gleefully ripped to shreds what we perceived as Verdi's primitive compositional techniques, especially compared to Wagner. More than twenty years later, however, I'm beginning to think at least some of our mirth was displaced.

Certainly, it cannot be directed at either of the operas under discussion here. *Don Carlos* continues the noble operatic tradition of existing in multiple editions; there are no fewer than *eight* different versions of the score (and two different ways to spell the title), although for our purposes we might reduce the count to three, any one of which you might confront in the opera house.

Verdi wrote *Don Carlos* for the Paris Opéra. Ever since the death of Meyerbeer, the French had been trying to entice Verdi back to the house for which he had written *Jérusalem* and *The Sicilian Vespers;* finally, with Schiller's dramatic poem *Don Carlos, Infant von Spanien* as the lure, they succeeded.

The first version of 1867 was in five acts and sung in French. Even before the premiere, however, the composer had to cut certain sections of this enormous historical grand opera, cuts that were not "opened" (in the hideous operatic parlance)—or indeed even discovered—until the critic Andrew Porter found the missing music pasted down in the orchestral parts stashed away at the Paris Opéra. Further whittling down ensued after the premiere and as the opera made its way to Italy.

But by 1884 it was clear that *Don Carlos* was not going to fly, operatically speaking, so Verdi revised it extensively, slicing away almost all of the first, or Fontainebleau, act, preserving only Carlos's aria, and translating it into Italian (thus: *Don Carlo*); it is in this form that the opera is probably best known. A compromise edition of 1886, known as the Modena version, restores the missing first act, but nowadays the trend, as noted above, is to return to the composer's first intentions, and the five-act French version is making a comeback.

Any way you do slice it—and in this case the original way is the best—*Don Carlos* is an epic masterpiece that ranks atop Verdi's finest work. The story concerns the Spanish prince (or *Infant,* in several Romance tongues) Carlos, grandson of the emperor Charles V, whose love for Elisabeth of Valois is unfortunately frustrated by her engagement, and later marriage, to his father, Philip II, the king of Spain. The opera explores a number of rich, complex themes, including the nature of friendship (between Carlos and Posa), the nature of love (between Carlos and Elisabeth, Elisabeth and Philip, Philip and Carlos, and Princess Eboli and Carlos, among others) and the nature of duty (the function of the Grand Inquisitor). Its centerpiece is a spectacular auto-da-fé scene that, alas, does not quite reach the heights of musical invention it should, being defaced by an incredibly stupid little brass tune at its midpoint.

Otherwise, no problems. Philip's battle of wills with the Inquisitor, in which public responsibility triumphs over personal feelings, is one of the opera's high points, as is the king's sorrowful aria, "Elle ne m'aime pas!" ("She never loved me after all!"), when he realizes that Elisabeth and Carlos still have a thing for each other. The Carlos-Posa "buddy" duet is a melodic bench mark (and it comes back poignantly at Posa's death), as are Eboli's big show tunes, the "Veil Song" and the aria "O don fatale."

Even the cop-out ending somehow seems to work. At the climax of Schiller's poem, Philip hands his renegade son over to the Inquisition; in the opera, Carlos seeks shelter from his father's vengeance in the monastery of Saint Just, where his old gramps had gone to spend the last of his days. Just as the soldiers are about to grab him, out shoots an arm from Charles V's tomb—is it a monk? the ghost of Chuck V himself? an outtake from a Brian de Palma movie?—which pulls Carlos to safety, or perdition, or wherever. Everybody is mystified, not least the audience.

With *Otello,* written between 1884 and 1886 (basically, the same period as the revisions of *Don Carlos*), Verdi raised his game to the next level and created an opera so perfect in form and function as to be the despair of all later composers. The mystery of *Otello* is one of the greatest in music history. Verdi felt he was washed up—too old, he said, too tired to compose anymore. But a bright young man named Arrigo Boito, a fine composer (*Mefistofele*) in his own right, kept knocking at the door, with a temptation that Verdi ultimately could not resist: a magnificent libretto based on Verdi's favorite playwright, Shakespeare. Boito's genius, no less than Verdi's, helped determine the outcome; reducing the play's 3,500 lines to something under 800, he nevertheless managed to preserve intact both the letter and the spirit of the play (proving once again that everybody can use an editor, even the Bard). The action is swift and to the point; scenes flow into each other with nary a break (there is only one onstage scene change, in Act III); nothing impedes the opera's forward motion to the final tragedy.

Verdi lavished upon this timeless material his most dramatic, affecting, and compelling music. From the Moor's blood-chilling cry of victory—"Esultate!"—to the final recollection of the first-act love duet, heard as Desdemona and the Moor lie dead and dying, *Otello* is a work of such majesty as to occupy, practically alone, a plane above all its rivals. Verdi's Iago is a sinister creature with his own villainous internal logic, and his "Credo" is a masterpiece of evil justifying its baleful existence; Desdemona is perhaps the loveliest creation in the Verdian pantheon, while the Moor dominates the stage in all his guises, whether as conquering hero or prostrate lover, cursed with jealousy.

Listen carefully to the end of Act III and, in a few bars, you will hear why *Otello* is so great. Otello lies on the floor, reduced to a writhing hunk of protoplasm by the schemes of Iago. Outside, the people are cheering his name; inside, he's a wreck. "Ecco il Leone!" exults the triumphant Iago, and the orchestra thunders out a dastardly cadence: E major to C major. This implicit clash of tonalities perfectly sums up the conflicting dramatic situations; rarely is a C-major ending less "happy" than this one. And what happens in the last act, we know too well: "I kiss'd thee ere I kill'd thee; no way but this, killing myself to die upon a kiss." *Otello* is, indeed, an opera to die for.

Georges Bizet: *Carmen.* And speaking of not-so-happy major-key endings—and unfinished masterpieces that exist in various versions—how about this one? Bizet's saucy little senorita is rightly accorded a place as the world's most popular opera (and a French opera at that), but that reputation has partially obscured what a wonderful work of art it is. Based on Prosper Mérimée's novella, the opera was composed for the Opéra-Comique in Paris, where it bombed, at least as far as Bizet's expectations were concerned, in March of 1875, perhaps precipitating the composer's untimely death at the age of thirty-six a few months later. Actually, *Carmen* got thirty-five performances that spring and thirteen more the next season, more than any of his earlier operas, such as *The Pearl Fishers,* had received, but the tale of *Carmen*'s hostile reception makes a nice story for those who believe in the starving-artist theory of cultural history.

Amazingly, the score was perceived by critics—those perspicacious critics again—as "scientific" and "Wagnerian" (the latter adjective was also applied to Verdi's *Aida* and *Otello,* for what it's worth), while the plot was deemed "immoral." Some of the musical numbers were certainly admired, but folks were understandably puzzled by a tragic opera at the Opéra-Comique ("No, Georges, it's supposed to be *funny*"), and a complex one at that. What was the Paris bourgeoisie to make of it?

Good question. Shortly after Bizet's death, Guiraud

(the same guy who was to fix *The Tales of Hoffmann* a few years later) composed recitatives to replace the spoken dialogue, and it was in this form that *Carmen* eventually made its way around the world. (Had he lived, Bizet apparently was going to do the same thing.) Naturally, today the "correct" way of performing *Carmen* is to eliminate the recits and perform the dialogue; the 1964 critical edition by Fritz Oeser also restores material that Bizet cut before and during rehearsals. Once again, though, the problem of the afterlife pops up: just as the Rimsky version of *Boris* may, in fact, be the more effective way of presenting Mussorgsky's vision, so *Carmen* is probably better—and, in a way, more "authentic"—with its recitatives instead of its dialogue. Another consideration that argues in favor of the recits is the difficulty of finding singers who know and can pronounce the French language convincingly. It's hard enough to find international singers at home in the French repertoire; it's almost impossible to find singers who can speak the words. The best solution is to mix bits and pieces of the original and Oeser versions and then make the best artistic case you can in performance.

By now, you may see a pattern emerging: why can't composers simply write down the notes they want performed and then leave the damn thing alone? Some contemporary creators do just that (which may be why their operas don't last very long), but to an experienced theater composer, it's just not that simple. You can propose, but performers and circumstances dispose. Arias have to be rewritten or cut entirely, ensembles rejiggered, choruses added or subtracted. Rarely is there a "definitive" edition of an opera or, for that matter, a Broadway show. (Think of *Show Boat,* which has more variant editions than *Boris Godunov.*) A musical, whatever its venue, is the product of trial and error, and undergoes constant revision. Tenor can't sing "Il mio tesoro"? Then write "Dalla sua pace" and get on with the show; if that way of working was good enough for Mozart, it's good enough for everybody. Eventually, if the opera or musical is successful, it finds a more or less final form. Subject to change without notice, of course.

What is it we love about *Carmen*? The many hit tunes, of course, such as the "Habañera" and the "Toreador Song," which are familiar to nearly everyone, no matter what his or her level of cultural sophistication. *Carmen* is one of the most melodically profligate scores in the history of opera, a succession of hit tunes the likes of which one would be hard pressed to discover in any other work.

But more than its airs, what we love about *Carmen* is its drama. Bizet and his librettists, Meilhac and Halévy, improved on Mérimée in many ways, not the least of which was by staging the final Don José–Carmen confrontation outside the bullring where Escamillo is fighting, instead of on a lonely road. They also invented the character of Micaëla, the stereotypical good-girl-next-door, as a foil for the feisty gypsy wench. Although lengthy, the opera moves swiftly from scene to scene, and there is hardly a note we would gladly do without. Bizet's music never merely ornaments the words, it drives them; from the first note of the famous overture to the last (very unhappy) major-key sonority, *Carmen* captivates us every bit as much as the title character enchants poor, luckless Don José.

Sopranos and mezzos love this part, and every great one has given it a shot. The list is nearly endless, but among the greatest interpreters of the roles have been Emma Calvé (maybe the sexiest Carmen in history), Mary Garden, Geraldine Farrar, Risë Stevens, Grace Bumbry, and Leontyne Price. The character is nearly inexhaustible—if ever there was a female Don Giovanni, who dies unrepentant for his or her life-style, it is Carmen, one of opera's great tragic heroines. She's the bad girl our moms warned us about, the one we—thank God—can't resist.

• • •

Alban Berg: *Wozzeck* and *Lulu.* And speaking of bad girls, how about that little tart Lulu, the heroine of a couple of Frank Wedekind plays and the eponymous Venus's-flytrap of Berg's second and last opera? She's bad news, that's for sure, dragging every man she meets down to perdition until she gets her just deserts (from Jack the Ripper, no less!) at the opera's end. In *Wozzeck,* meanwhile, the hero is a card-carrying member of the lumpen proletariat, a miserable sod who is abused by the Captain, tortured by the Doctor, beat up by the Drum Major, and cuckolded by his girlfriend, Marie (by whom he has an illegitimate child), all of which mistreatment finally drives him to murder and suicide.

Sounds like just the kind of operas you might want to stage for, say, Jesse Helms and the Family Values Coalition, right? Which brings up the question: how come opera concerns itself so often with the lowest sort of behavior: rape, murder, incest, etc.? Why can't there be "nice" operas about, well . . . about nuns? There are. Puccini's *Suor Angelica* is about a young girl who gives birth to an illegitimate child, enters a convent, and then, overcome with remorse after she learns of the child's death, kills herself by drinking poison. (But it has a happy ending: the BVM herself appears to lead Angelica to heaven anyway.) Oops! Well, how about Poulenc's *Dialogues of the Carmelites,* which takes place during the French Revolution: at its climax the members of the order—an amazing assortment of unhappy, maladjusted, dysfunctional women—are guillotined one by one. Okay, maybe not nuns then. . . .

The point is, goody-two-shoes subjects are not exactly catnip for composers. (For the same reason that good-news newspapers don't sell.) Maybe Tolstoy was right: all happy families are alike, but each unhappy family is unhappy in its own way. The whole point of art—which has totally escaped the morons behind NEA bashing—is to examine the deepest nature of human beings, which may or may not be good, or may or may not be base. But opera composers and other creative artists know something that those whose weltanschauung seems to have been formed by *Father Knows Best* and *Ozzie and Harriet* do not: that at its root, the human character is fundamentally amoral. Please do not take this as a plea for perversity. But perversity is, to a large extent, in the cultural context of the beholder.

Which is why we have so many apparently amoral characters in opera. I say apparently because in opera these rape survivors, child molestors, incestuous siblings, et alia are *not bad people.* They are, in fact, a lot like you and me; they are, in fact, perfectly normal, within the operatic context. That's why we find them so fascinating.

A word about operatic context. Obviously, opera is not meant to be about "real life." Today, we no longer seem capable of understanding something that used to go without saying: "It's only a movie" (or an opera, or a play, or a musical). Just because *Show Boat* originally opened with the line "Niggers all work on de Mississippi" doesn't make it racist; if anything, *Show Boat* is profoundly liberal on the subject of racism. But to go to the trouble of listening to it carefully is clearly too much work for knee-jerk reactionaries, who would condemn a classic of American musical theater on the basis of one word of the libretto. (Have they listened to the dialogue in *Menace II Society*, one wonders.) It's probably only a matter of time before the same Kultur Nazis discover that *The Marriage of Figaro* is about an aristocrat who demands the right to sleep with the new wife of his manservant, or that *The Magic Flute* portrays a black character unsympathetically.

In the same way, those who would censor art on the basis of its content are out to lunch. Art is supposed to deal with tricky matters of manners and mores; that's its job. Art is not supposed to be comfortable; art is not something that is supposed to make you feel better about your raggedy-assed, miserable, no-good, worthless self. Instead, it's supposed to make you examine the reason *why* you're miserable, no good, and raggedy-assed, and to understand it.

Thus Wedekind, Berg, and *Lulu*. If Wedekind, an outrageous avant-gardist with whose attitudes and presentation Karen Finley would feel right at home, were to have come before the Endowment seeking support for his work, he would never make it in today's climate. And yet his plays, *Pandora's Box* and *Earth-Spirit,* not only provided the substance for Berg's masterpiece, they also provided the vehicle for a memorable Louise Brooks–G. W. Pabst cinematic collaboration. Are Wedekind's plays "immoral" (the same adjective, recall, that was applied to *Carmen* and, even earlier, to Mozart's *Don Giovanni*)? If they are, can moral works of art (Berg's opera, Pabst's film) emerge from them? If so, how? If not, why not?

Tough issues. But that's another of the things we love about opera.

So let's get down to cases. Lulu is that operatic staple, the femme fatale. Everybody who comes in contact with her—including Alwa the composer; his father, Dr. Schön; a doctor, a painter, Schigolch (who or may not be her father), the lesbian Countess Geschwitz, the Athlete, and the Schoolboy—falls in love with her and, one way or another, most of them wind up being destroyed by her. (In a nice twist of the doubling of roles, the actor who takes the nonsinging role of the doctor comes back at the end as Jack the Ripper.)

Wozzeck, the put-upon soldier, similarly wreaks havoc, although it is limited to his own immediate circle. Tortured beyond endurance, both psychologically and physically (the libretto is based on the extraordinary play by Georg Büchner, an early-nineteenth-century German playwright), he eventually turns not on his tormentors but on his own, slitting Marie's throat with a knife and then drowning as he wades into a lake, insanely seeking to recover the murder weapon.

Berg's musical language in these two operas is quite different. *Wozzeck,* the earlier of the two, is more or less atonal—that is, is has no fixed key center—but when discussing Berg, "more or less" are always the operative words. Berg was a student and disciple of Schoenberg, and revered his master, but was a far greater humanist—and a far greater composer. Schoenberg's operas are abstractions: *Erwartung* (*Expectation*) is a symbolist one-acter; *Moses und Aron* a stylized, undramatic lecture. Berg's are about real people and his art, however intellectually based, is always at the service of emotion. For the final orchestral interlude (between Scenes 4 and 5 of Act III), Berg unabashedly adopts the key of D minor in which to compose his threnody on the deaths of Wozzeck and Marie; few moments in all opera rise to the emotional heights of this passage, one of the most renowned and affecting in contemporary music.

In *Lulu,* Berg adopted Schoenberg's famous (or infamous) twelve-tone system. Berg had composed one of *Wozzeck*'s scenes with the twelve-tone system; now, in *Lulu,* he employed it on a massive scale. Twelve-tone music is commonly adjudged to be "difficult" but, oddly, *Lulu* has proven to be a more popular work than *Wozzeck,* for reasons I am at a loss to explain. *Lulu* is far, far longer and much denser, but its story line is clearer (and less German expressionistic), and everyone seems to identify with the story of an amoral temptress who finally gets her well-deserved comeuppance in the end.

Both operas repay careful listening and careful analysis. Berg was a numerologist, and he peppered his music with hidden structures, references, and meanings. He was also obsessed with form: *Wozzeck*'s three acts are divided into "Five Character Pieces," a "Symphony in Five Movements," and "Six Inventions," one of them being the famous D-minor interlude. *Lulu* shows a similar eye for internal structures.

Lulu is also—to pick up another theme of our discussion so far—unfinished. Or, rather, was. On Christmas Eve, 1935, Berg died of blood poisoning, caused by complications of a bee sting, and although he left the opera substantially complete in what composers call the "short score" (that is, a piano score with some orchestrational details), most of the orchestration of the third act was still to come. There should have been little problem in preparing the opera for performance, but by 1935 Berg was already on the Nazis' anathema list as a composer of *entartete Kunst* (decadent art). Later his widow, Helene, actively obstructed all efforts to get at Act III, possibly because she felt Berg had squirreled away some secret references to a love affair he was having at the time. (Berg's *Lyric Suite,* we now know, is a secret ode to his mistress, so Helene may have had good grounds for suspicion.) *Lulu* was therefore heard in a truncated version (the first two acts and a bit of the third) until Frau Berg died in 1976, after which the Viennese composer Friedrich Cerha finished the orchestration and the full score was finally premiered in 1979 in Paris by Pierre Boulez. Today, the full three-act *Lulu* is the only way the opera is—or should ever be—staged.

Pretty intimidating, you say. So why should you trust your tender ears to Berg's acerbic sonorities, just on my say-so? You don't have to, of course. And I would be very surprised if 10 percent of the readers of this book eventually come to love either of Berg's naughty problem children. And yet, just as much as Mozart or Verdi or Wagner, Berg is a part of the operatic continuum, and his operas—both indisputable masterpieces—will be performed as long as opera still holds the stage. You may have to stretch your ears a bit to wrap them around some of the music, but the effort will be more than amply repaid. In the end, you'll be glad you did.

Scott Joplin: *Treemonisha.* Why isn't this fine work from the pen of one of America's most famous, and least-understood, composers better known? Perhaps I am about to engage in some special pleading for a flawed, inexpert work; so sue me. But I would be remiss were I not to bring *Treemonisha* to your attention, and not just for its wonderful finale, "A Real Slow Drag."

Joplin is, to my mind, the greatest of all nineteenth-century American composers, both for the magnitude of his achievement and the scope of his effort. (You who scoff: name the competition. MacDowell?) You undoubtedly know him as the King of the Ragtime Writers (as he was called in his lifetime), and the composer of the "Maple Leaf Rag." But Joplin was far more, and far greater. He was an American archetype, the first great synthesizer of the European classical- and American popular-music traditions, the haphazardly educated son of a freed slave who welded the music and dance of black America to the simple European forms (march, two-step, waltz) that had found wide popularity across the country in the late nineteenth-century and so created the country's first great vernacular music.

Joplin's success with the "Maple Leaf Rag" in 1899—unlike most composers, who sold their works outright, Joplin received a one-cent royalty on each copy sold—gave him a measure of financial stability that was welcome after his years laboring in the demimonde as a bordello pianist. (The young Brahms was a whorehouse "perfesser" for a time, as well.) In the first decade of the new twentieth century, he turned out classic rag after classic piano rag, including the "Gladiolus Rag," which may be his finest piano work.

But Joplin longed for more. His ambition was nothing less than to be taken seriously as a serious composer. What a preposterous notion! A black man, whose formal musical education consisted of some courses at the George R. Smith College for Negroes in Sedalia, Mo., presuming to exalt himself to a level reserved for White Europeans. Surely he jested.

Surely, not. With the encouragement of Alfred Ernst, a German conductor resident in America, he set out to compose an opera. As Monroe H. Rosenfeld, a popular composer of the day, wrote in a 1903 newspaper article about Joplin:

> *Joplin's ambition is to shine in other spheres. . . . To this end he is assiduously toiling upon an opera, nearly a score of the numbers of which he has already composed and which he hopes to give an early production [in St. Louis].*

The opera in question was not *Treemonisha* but something called *A Guest of Honor,* and it makes a tantalizing story. It was apparently performed once, in St. Louis; according to Arthur Marshall, one of Joplin's fellow ragtime composers and friends, "It was taken quite well and I think [Joplin] was about to get Haviland or Majestic Producers to handle or finance the play, also book it. I can't say just how far it got."

Nowhere, is how far. Although the opera was registered at the Library of Congress, no copy of the score was ever received, and *A Guest of Honor* has seemingly vanished. From time to time, rumors of its existence crop up—found in a bank safe in Carson City, or Nevada City, or the Emerald City—but no one has ever actually seen a copy. I have a theory, though: what if Joplin gave a copy of the score to Ernst (not unlikely); what if Ernst took it back to Germany with him (ditto); what if he stored it with his papers at his home in Halle (a certainty, given points one and two); and what if it survived the wartime bombing of the East German city (debatable)? Is it possible that *A Guest of Honor* might turn up in Halle? I think it's our best bet.

Joplin returned to writing rags, but the opera bug never left him. After his move to New York City in 1909, he set about working on *Treemonisha,* and by 1911 the score was ready. Unfortunately, no one wanted to publish it, not even Joplin's longtime publisher John Stark, who had folded his business on Tin Pan Alley the year before and returned to St. Louis. So Joplin published *Treemonisha* at his own expense, an act of folly that finished him financially and emotionally.

No one wanted to perform it. *Treemonisha* was not the first opera on a black subject by an African-American composer—that honor belongs to *The Martyr* by Harry Lawrence Freeman, which was produced in Denver in 1893—but it was the most significant, and Joplin knew it. In 1913 he and his wife, Lottie, moved uptown, to Harlem, where he worked on revising some of the numbers (not for the better, it should be noted) and organized the opera's one and only performance, a costumeless run-through that took place in a rented Harlem hall, called the Lincoln Theater, in 1915. Unable to afford the services of an orchestra, Joplin himself played the piano.

It was a flop, and it killed him. (Shades of Bizet, only this time with more historical accuracy.) Joplin was dying from tertiary syphilis, and the failure of *Treemonisha* drove him over the edge, into madness; he died at the Manhattan State Hospital on Wards Island, in the East River, on April 1, 1917. Our story, however, has a happy ending. In 1975, *Treemonisha* was finally staged, in Houston, and it went on to win the Pulitzer Prize for music that year.

The plot concerns the efforts of Treemonisha, a foundling girl child, to lead the recently freed slaves in the area of Texarkana, Arkansas (near where Joplin grew up), out of ignorance and superstition and into the light of education and reason. The libretto was Joplin's own, and it reflected his beliefs. Only through education, he felt, could the Negro take his place alongside the white man in America, and Treemonisha's battle with the wicked conjurers was his vivid image for the struggle for the soul of black America.

Joplin was an inexperienced stage composer—his earlier folk ballet, *The Ragtime Dance,* had not been a success, and *Treemonisha* is an admittedly difficult proposition to stage. For one thing, the original orchestrations are long since lost, and most performances have used those of Gunther Schuller. The libretto strikes us today as inexpert and naïve. A more serious flaw is the work's reliance on picturesque scene painting at the expense of real dramatic engagement.

Still, it hardly matters whether *Treemonisha* ever enters the repertoire, for the music lives on. "A Real Slow Drag," the final celebratory dance, is one of Joplin's most inspired compositions, as well as one of the most effective and uplifting operatic finales ever written, but many of the other numbers are equally fine, including the rousing "Aunt Dinah Has Blowed de Horn"; the amazingly avant-garde ensemble called "Confusion," with its chorus of indeterminate pitches depicting the lamentations of the plantation women; and the radiant anthem "We Will Trust You as Our Leader."

Treemonisha deserves an honored place in American music history—not for any fuzzy reasons of affirmative action, but because it is an astonishing masterpiece that has no counterpart elsewhere. You owe it to Joplin to seek a score for which he literally gave his life, but more important, you owe it to your country and yourself.

Leoš Janáček: *Jenůfa.* With Verdi, we saw that very great operas could be written by very old people. Surprise, surprise. But with the Czech composer Leoš Janáček, we see something far more noteworthy: that one's first great work could be written very late in life. Talk about the Golden Years; Janáček (say YAHN-na-check) is their embodiment.

Before we get into *Jenůfa* proper—if you really want to show off, give it its real title, *Její Pastorkyňa* (*Her Foster-Daughter*)—a few words are in order about Janáček's particular, and peculiar, sense of harmony and melody. Janáček, who was born in Moravia in 1854, was a dedicated Czech patriot who battled fiercely against German cultural hegemony, explicitly ignoring Prague's German-language theater in favor of the theater that performed in Czech. (The Czech provinces of Bohemia and Moravia traditionally have been heavily influenced by their powerful neighbor.) Most of his works have something to do with Czech history or folklore, but even more important, they partake part and parcel of the rhythms and inflections of the Czech tongue. Indeed, they are unthinkable without it.

So what? Can't operas be translated easily from one language into another, the same way novels can? Ignoring the issue of whether novels can make a seamless transition from, say, Russian to French (they can't), the answer is unequivocally no. The way a composer sets the words of a libretto—and in opera there is no question that, unlike the way some songwriters work, fitting a melody to newly cobbled lyrics, the words come first in order of creation—is determined (if the composer is any good) by the natural inflections of the language itself.

Let's take an example. In Hungarian, for example, the stress is quite regular, since every word is accented on the first syllable. French, on the other hand, has a high percentage of words whose accent falls on the last syllable, while German and English are all over the map. It may seem like a small thing, but over the course of a four-hundred-page score, the displaced accents, false stresses, and other horrors that attend opera in translation add up.

So the best way to listen to Janáček (or to any opera, for that matter) is in the original. For Janáček, like his fellow Slav Mussorgsky, was incredibly conscious of composing melodic lines that fit the natural shape of his native speech; in fact, one way to look at his music is as a highly developed alternative form of the Czech language.

Harmonically, too, Janáček is unusual. It's hard to explain exactly why, but two minutes of listening to a Janáček score and you will understand what I mean.

Maybe it's because he found his mature style so late in life (the bulk of his famous works were composed after he turned sixty-five), or maybe it's simply because he was a genius, but Janáček's music sounds as if a Martian was trying to write nineteenth-century tonal music. It's right—but not quite right. There is just enough "wrong" to set it apart from the run of the mill. Janáček's chord progressions never seem to go where you expect them to; what may start as a conventional harmonic rhythm will suddenly veer off into something totally surprising and original. Janáček's music demands attention—not because it's so innately complicated but because it's so delightfully quirky. Maybe that's the wrong word. It sounds too flippant, as if Janáček were humorous. Strange his music sometimes is, but it is far more: deep, heartfelt, passionate.

In *Jenůfa,* his first great opera (and his first performed opera, for that matter, although he had written others), Janáček found a story worthy of his talents. The plot concerns the title heroine, a rural girl who has been made pregnant by her cousin, the toper Steva (say SHTAY-va). But her stern, pitiless stepmother, called the Kostelnička (the title—Ko-stel-NITS-ka—means a female sacristan), frowns on the union; meanwhile, Steva's half-brother, Laca (pronounced LAT-sa), who is also in love with Jenůfa, is jealous and, as the first act ends, he slashes the beautiful Jenůfa's face with a knife, disfiguring her.

Act II begins five months later. The unmarried Jenůfa has given birth to a son in secret, and is now sleeping. The Kostelnička tries to get Steva to make an honest woman of Jenůfa, but no dice. The next visitor is Laca, who still loves her (although he certainly has a funny way of showing his affection), but he is so alarmed when he learns Jenůfa has had a child that the Kostelnička hurriedly tells him that the child is dead—a statement she makes come true after he leaves by throwing the baby into the nearest icy stream. When Jenůfa wakes up and wonders where her son is, the Kostelnička tells her the child has died of a fever. The mollified Laca returns, proposes, and is accepted without enthusiasm. The last scene of the act belongs to the Kostelnička; as an eerie wind howls outside, her conscience begins to afflict her and the evil woman cowers in terror before the elements.

The last act opens with the preparations for the Jenůfa-Laca nuptials, which are quickly spoiled by the discovery of the little frozen corpse. The open-minded villagers are about to lynch poor Jenůfa when the Kostelnička suddenly 'fesses up and gets dragged away to justice. It is left to Jenůfa (apparently, the only intelligent person in the village) to forgive her wicked stepmother and to come to terms with her love—such as it is—for Laca, and the opera ends.

A strange, equivocal story, but rendered incredibly powerful through the force of Janáček's innovative inspiration. For it is the composer who gives moral shape and meaning to the story through his marvelous music; it is the composer who tells us how we should feel about the characters; it is the composer who makes us care about these unlovely, bigoted people; it is the composer who makes sense of their (to us) alien universe; it is the composer who, in the end, makes convincing Jenůfa's almost incredible magnanimity. In short, it is the composer who makes the story—human.

Dmitri Shostakovich: *Lady Macbeth of the Mtsensk District.* Which brings us to another opera about exotic and naughty Slavs, one that offended the most powerful man in the evil empire. Talk about bad reviews: Dmitri Shostakovich's second opera enraged no less a critic than Uncle Joe Stalin his own bad self, a notice that changed the course of the composer's life and, perhaps, that of modern operatic history as well.

What frosted the Leader and Teacher so badly that *Pravda* (the Russian word for "truth") carried an editorial in 1936 that denounced the opera as "Muddle Instead of

Music"? What didn't? Almost everything about *Lady Macbeth* was, intentionally or not, sure to offend the stuffy Soviet hierarchy. The story concerns a frustrated housewife, Katerina Ismailova, who cuckolds her boring husband, Zinovy, with the day laborer Sergei; poisons her suspicious, meddlesome father-in-law with a dinner of lethal mushrooms; and beats Zinovy to death with a candlestick. She and Sergei are about to marry when hubby's body is discovered rotting away in the cellar by a local drunk. Under arrest and on the road to Siberia, she is betrayed by Sergei, who takes up with another woman; enraged, Katerina pushes his new girlfriend into a river, and then jumps in herself.

In other words, just another day at the beach in old Mother Russia.

Here again, we are confronted with a singular cast of non-role models. And yet, as we've noted before, not only are we *not* supposed to condemn these people for their behavior, we are supposed to be *sympathetic* to them and their problems. Because the composer wants us to.

In Nikolai Leskov's 1865 short story *Ledi Makbet Mtsenskovo uyezda,* the protagonists are treated ironically; Katerina is a cruel bitch with no redeeming social values. Shostakovich, however, saw the material as an opportunity to make a larger moral—and political—point. "As a Soviet composer," he wrote in 1934, the year of *Lady Macbeth*'s premiere, "I determined to preserve the strength of Leskov's novel, and yet, approaching it critically, to interpret its events from our modern point of view." The mid-1930s were perilous times for all Soviet citizens, but in particular for Stalin's opponents, whether real or imagined. The midnight knock at the door and the muffled pistol shot in the back alley were things to be feared; no one knew when disfavor might arrive. Artists were especially wary, since they were expected to carry on the fight for Soviet communism through their works: "formalism" was out; "socialist realism" was in.

Now, what were formalism and socialist realism? Basically, they were anything the Soviet censors said they were. The list of no-nos included anything that smacked of the twelve-tone system, of course, and most of the other advanced techniques of Western composition at the time. At the same time, good socialist art was supposed to reflect the hopes, dreams, and aspirations of the People. Operas that depicted various low-lifes involved in adultery and murder were very definitely not what Marx and Lenin had in mind, and how Shostakovich could have thought they were is one of opera history's little mysteries.

The strange thing is that it took almost two years before anyone figured that out. At first the opera was a hit, considered not only a worthy successor to the composer's first opera, the satirical *The Nose,* but a distinct improvement on it. *Lady Macbeth* was produced across the Soviet Union and outside the country as well. Then Stalin happened to attend a performance in December 1935 and that was the end of that; the next month the infamous editorial appeared—unsigned, but everybody knew who was calling the shots—and *Lady Macbeth* vanished from the repertoire overnight. "Is its success abroad not explained by the fact that it tickles the perverted bourgeois taste with its fidgety, screaming, neurotic music?" wondered *Pravda.* You bet!

The effect on Shostakovich was profound. The gentle, reclusive composer was shattered. In fear for his life, Shostakovich abjectly apologized by not only yanking *Lady Macbeth* but his new Fourth Symphony as well; the celebrated Fifth Symphony of 1937 was subtitled "a Soviet composer's response to just criticism." Nearly thirty years later, well after Stalin was six feet under, Shostakovich revised his problem child, issuing a bowdlerized version of the score as *Katerina Ismailova,* and it was in this form that the opera was most often performed until after the composer's death in 1975.

So here we have both our main issues: culpable characters and alternate performing editions. As to the latter, it is no contest: *Lady Macbeth* can truly be said to exist in only one version, the first. There are some who admire *Katerina,* but she came to life only under duress, a nice-Nancy version of her older, hotter sister.

Regarding the former, we note the irony that lumps together murderous godless Communists and the Moral Majority in their distaste for matters sexual—strange bedfellows indeed! When Shostakovich, faced with a force majeure, revised his opera, he tossed out the most offending passages, including the extremely explicit depiction of Sergei and Katerina's first coupling (the detumescent trombone licks never fail to elicit titters from the audience). But to remove those is to cut out the heart of the opera, which is, after all, about the consequences of sexual frustration and unbridled passion.

Once again, it's important to understand that Shostakovich is not necessarily arguing in *favor* of licentiousness. Instead, the artist is forcing us to examine these appetites in light of our own moral codes. They may be strange and evil, or appealing and seductive, but however we choose to see them, they are a part of our world. The real artist subscribes fully to the old Latin motto, "Nothing human is foreign to me." *Lady Macbeth* forces us to look at our own passions and wonder whether we might be capable of the same excesses as well. And if not, why not.

Richard Strauss: *Salome, Elektra,* and *Der Rosenkavalier.* And speaking of excesses . . .

Richard Strauss was one of the most important composers and musical figures of the second half of the nineteenth century and the first half of the twentieth (he died in 1949), and in these operas he contributed to the repertoire three of the most thrilling works ever written.

He wrote much more, of course, and you can get into a fight with Straussians if you offhandedly dismiss most of the operas that came after *Ariadne auf Naxos*—with *Die Frau ohne Schatten, Arabella,* and *Capriccio* as possible exceptions—as second rate. However, they are, so there's no point in wasting time with the likes of *The Egyptian Helen* and *Daphne* and other such dreck.

Instead, let's get right to the good stuff. Strauss was already a renowned composer of tone poems by the time he turned his attention toward opera in his two warmups, *Guntram* and *Feuersnot.* Then he got his hands on a German translation of Oscar Wilde's French-language drama *Salome,* and the rest is history. Adapting the play himself, Strauss fashioned a full-length, one-act opera of such seething sexuality and raw passion that it was informally banned for a time in both Britain and, after its premiere at the Met, in the United States as well. (Artur Rubinstein recounts in his memoirs that he used to play the forbidden score on the piano privately for Edward VII.) "I like this fellow Strauss," said the kaiser, "but *Salome* will do him a lot of damage." To which Strauss retorted that the opera had allowed him to build his villa in Garmisch.

Strauss followed up the scandal of *Salome* with another shocker, *Elektra,* which also represented the beginning of an extraordinarily fruitful collaboration with the poet and librettist Hugo von Hofmannsthal. Hofmannsthal had adapted Sophocles for his own dramatic version of the Greek tragedy, and when Strauss came calling he had just the ticket for another one-act opera.

I assume that everybody knows about John the Baptist's head on a silver platter and what happened to the House of Atreus after Agamemnon took that darn bath. Suffice it to say that the plots adhere closely to the famous stories. But Strauss did not merely set them to music: he transformed them into higher beings through musical means. From the outset of both operas, he ratchets up the tension, both musical and dramatic, with his edgy, darting music: the lascivious clarinet lick that opens *Salome,* the thundering "Agamemnon" motif that kicks off *Elektra.* Once you start either work, you have to listen straight through to the end: the seamlessness of their construction—the only "stop-the-opera" showpiece comes in *Salome*'s "Dance of the Seven Veils"—makes it impossible to stop.

Up to this point in his career, Strauss had been a relatively well-behaved representative of late romanticism. Even his huge orchestral works, like the *Symphonia domestica* and *An Alpine Symphony,* conformed to Wagnerian models. But in *Salome* and *Elektra* something happened; these are works that angle toward the harsh expressionism of Schoenberg and Berg without ever quite getting there. It is a cliché to say that Strauss approached the abyss of atonality and flinched, and maybe he did. But so what? Atonality would not have made these two miracles one whit more powerful than they already are.

And then he stepped back—all the way back to the spirit of eighteenth-century Vienna, with *Der Rosenkavalier.* Surely the best-loved German opera in the repertoire, it is also one of the most perfect operas ever composed. Hofmannsthal's libretto may be too good for its own good, but its wordplay is piquant, especially if you understand German, and in the characters of Octavian, the young knight of the Silver Rose; Sophie, the ingenue; and the Marschallin, the wife of a field commander with whom Octavian is having an affair, he gave us three operatic immortals.

Rosenkavalier was a deliberate throwback, even down to the casting of a mezzo-soprano as Octavian (one of opera's so-called pants roles). The sexual byplay in this opera is something to behold; at one point the girl singing the boy Octavian must dress up as a girl, so she/he/she can be ogled by Baron Ochs. Such confusion or masking of sexual identity has been a staple of opera since its origins: in opera, some really do like it hot, and obviously Strauss and Hofmannsthal numbered themselves among them.

Musically, the opera is far more approachable than either of its fiery sisters; the anachronistic waltzes (the waltz was not invented until the nineteenth century) long ago became concert favorites, and the final trio attains heights of tonal-based expression and emotion that were never to be reached again. The whole work is nothing but artifice and yet it moves us every time, thanks to Strauss's skill in finding exactly the right musical means with which to tell his story. No one can come away from *Der Rosenkavalier* without a tear in the eye or a catch in the throat, and even a century of saccharine Germanic sentimentalization—come on, the Marschallin is not seventy-five years old—has not ruined its appeal. German opera doesn't come any friendlier than this, even if it is in drag.

Claudio Monteverdi: *The Coronation of Poppea.* Return with me now to those glorious days of yesteryear, to the moral Golden Age of Imperial Rome, when men were men but sometimes they dressed up like ladies and . . .

No, stop! Don't tell me you're going to recommend yet another opera about transvestites and perverts!

Sorry, Charlie, but we're going to have a closer look at the earliest opera in the standard repertoire, to put these thorny questions of moral fiber and alternative editions to rest once and for all.

Poppea, Monteverdi's last opera, was premiered during the Venetian Carnival season of 1642 or 1643. It was frankly written to attract an audience, being presented in a theater and not at court. It is also the first opera to use a historical subject, set in Rome in the year A.D. 62. Poppea is a woman of uncommon charms, who has attracted the attentions of no less a personage than Emperor Nero himself. As the opera begins, Poppea's former lover, Ottone, returns from the wars to find his best babe shacked up with the boss. Ottone curses Poppea for her fickleness, and his complaints are echoed by the soldiers who stand watch outside Poppea's house, guarding the emperor while he fiddles with his new love. Poppea, realizing her hold over Nero, asks him to ditch the empress, Octavia, but the statesman Seneca counsels him against it. For his troubles, he is condemned to commit suicide at the behest of Nero, who is naturally encouraged in this decision by Poppea. Ottone has been thinking about murdering Poppea, but decides instead to take up with her friend Drusilla, who is secretly in love with him. Then Octavia summons Ottone and commands him to kill her rival, Poppea, but in order to do this he has to dress up as a woman, so naturally he goes to Drusilla to borrow her clothes and of course she readily agrees. Meanwhile . . .

Enough, already! It sounds less like an opera plot than an average episode of *Baywatch* or *As the World Turns.* Monteverdi's audience, however, would have been quite familiar with the story and would not for a minute have been put off by its shocking immorality. Nor would they have objected to the fact that the virile Nero was probably portrayed by a castrato. Indeed, back then, men commonly took women's roles, and women took men's; Monteverdi's audiences wouldn't have worried at all about the complex issues of transvestism and sexual identity, over which modern society expends so much energy.

The only two extant scores of *Poppea* are remarkably bare-boned: just the voice parts and a single bass line, sometimes with a so-called figured bass indication, the implication being that singers and a small continuo of organ, harpsichord or harp, and gamba basically would be enough. (Figured bass is musical shorthand, a bass note with two numbers written above it, usually 6-4 or 6-3, indicating the intervals that the player should fill in above the note.) For years, everyone assumed that Monteverdi must have meant for *Poppea* to be played with more instruments, and revivals were often outfitted with strings and trumpets. Recent scholarship, however, tends to believe that for economic reasons Monteverdi called for much smaller forces than would have been at his disposal thirty-five years earlier at the Mantuan court: *Poppea* was created for the public theater and reflected the need to cut costs and make a profit. There is also the issue of how much of the music was actually composed by Monteverdi. Baroque experts have divined the presence of material by Cavalli and Francesco Sacrati.

Whatever the case, though, what we have in *Poppea* is opera's first great masterpiece, and for a number of reasons. First and foremost, it is ravishingly gorgeous. Don't be put off by the lack of familiar nineteenth-century guideposts—how was Monteverdi to know that Puccini would be coming along?—but listen instead to the purity and beauty of the melodies, and how they reflect the emotional states of the characters. This is an opera about the triumph of Love, and indeed the goddesses Fortuna, Virtù, and Amor, along with Pallas Athena, Mercury, and Venus, all play leading roles in the action; Monteverdi's music leaves no doubt as to whose side the composer is on. The final Nero-Poppea duet, a shameless ode to the joys of physical love, is one of the most ecstatic in operatic history.

All the other reasons, including its place in music history and what it tells us about the tastes of the seventeenth-century Italian audiences, are secondary. Listen to *Poppea* for its celebration of Eros, and not as a moral cautionary tale. For yes, the bad guys win: Ottone and Drusilla are banished and Octavia is driven into exile. As the opera ends, Poppea weds Nero as Amor and Venus look on with satisfaction. Love, or at least Lust, really does conquer all, whether you like it or not.

Benjamin Britten: *Death in Venice.* Benjamin Britten's valedictory work, and his greatest. League of Decency Alert: the dreaded homosexuals are about to come out of the closet and get up on the stage, singin' 'n dancin'.

Britten, of course, was one of Britain's leading composers—and gay. In a country where homosexuality at the time was (a) widespread and (b) traditional but (c) illegal and (d) severely punished, Britten lived quite openly with his longtime companion, the tenor Peter Pears. Just as openly, his operas and other dramatic works reflected his predilections. *Peter Grimes,* his first great stage masterpiece, concerns a funny old East Anglian fisherman whose boy assistants have a way of perishing; *Albert Herring* is about a greengrocer's lad who is crowned Queen of the May; *Billy Budd,* a kind of warmup for *Death in Venice,* is a frankly eroticized portrait of Melville's beautiful sailor lad; *Gloriana* is an opera written for the coronation of a queen (Elizabeth II) about a queen (Elizabeth I).

And yet "dear old Ben" was something of a beloved figure in Gay Old England and in fact became an institution in his later years. To this day, he is venerated by the British—consult any recent opera book published in England and the Britten chapter is as long as those on Verdi or Wagner—who, having relatively little to boast about musically, have taken to exaggerating the modest talents of composers like (for example) the pretentious and opaque Michael Tippett.

Britten is more than a cut above Tippett, and in his best operas—*Grimes, Billy Budd,* and *Death in Venice* are the three most likely to survive—he achieves real greatness. And of the three, his swan song, based on the novella by Thomas Mann, is the best. Written in 1971–72, when the composer was already seriously ill (he died in 1976), the opera was intended as a tribute to Pears, and although Britten was too sick to attend the premiere in 1973, he did finally manage to hear his friend in the role of Aschenbach two years later.

The libretto, by Myfanwy Piper, is a brilliant reduction of Mann's emotionally and morally complex story, and Britten responded to it with a depth of feeling and consummate command of musical technique. Like *Hoffmann,* the opera has multiple roles for a bass-baritone, representing the various nemeses Aschenbach encounters on his literal journey from Munich to Venice, and his moral journey from bourgeois morality to unfettered hedonism, which results in his symbolic journey from health to sickness to death. (Surely some enterprising stage director is even now planning a reinterpretation in which Aschenbach succumbs not to cholera but to AIDS.)

Britten pulls out all the stops. The moody Sea Interludes of *Grimes* are evoked in the music that accompanies Aschenbach's boat trip across the lagoon to La Serenissima, while the dance music that accompanies Tadzio, the Polish boy with whom the writer falls in love, evokes the spirit of earlier works such as *Gloriana* and *A Midsummer Night's Dream*. Aschenbach's own music—tremulous, hesitant, insecure, troubled at first, then becoming more passionate and finally, resigned—is Britten's most effective dramatic creation.

Just as Janáček does in *Jenůfa,* Britten works the operatic miracle of making all of us—straight or gay—care about the feelings of his central character. Aschenbach's lust for Tadzio seems not at all perverse or perverted, but natural and, while pathetic, rather sweet. Few images are more striking than that of the freshly rouged and barbered Aschenbach trying desperately to catch the eye of a boy who couldn't care less whether he even exists. At this point, the story transcends its literal homosexual tendencies and becomes the universal story of a man (Aschenbach, Don José, Hoffmann, Werther, et al.) who destroys himself for love, and steps lively to his doom.

Pietro Mascagni: *Cavalleria rusticana;* **Ruggiero Leoncavallo:** *Pagliacci.* Fools for love that we are, so are we often killers for it as well. The famous coupling of *Cav 'n Pag* offers two object lessons in why not to get carried away by mad passion.

Both one-act operas are also, despite the best efforts of their otherwise obscure composers, one-shot successes.

Pietro Mascagni and Ruggiero Leoncavallo labored mightily to overcome the curse of their early success, to no avail. How often do you hear (or have you ever heard of) such Mascagni wonders as *L'amico Fritz, Guglielmo Ratcliff, Iris, Le maschere, Isabeau, Parisina, Lodoletta,* and *Il piccolo Marat?* (Only the first on this list of losers is performed at all.) As for Leoncavallo, he went on to write *La bohème* (yes, the same story as Puccini's—how's that for a suicide mission?), *Zazà* and *Edipo re.*

So let us give thanks for the two operas that did go right. The stories are familiar: an affair, a pregnancy, and a fatal duel of honor in Sicily and some extra-marital hanky-panky in Calabria add up to textbook illustrations of the short-lived operatic movement known as *verismo* (realism) that flourished toward the end of the nineteenth century. In fact, these two operas pretty much *are* verismo, and we couldn't ask for two finer, or more enjoyable, examples.

Cavalleria came first, composed by the young Mascagni as his entry in the publisher Sonzogno's second opera-writing contest. He wrote it quickly, but got cold feet when it can time to submit it and decided to send in the fourth act of *Guglielmo Ratcliff* instead. Fortunately, his wife had more sense, and it was she who entered *Cavalleria.*

It won big. With amazing speed, the opera rocketed around the globe, making the name Mascagni an operatic household word. First performed in 1890, the opera was heard in the United States and Britain the following year. Mascagni was the John Grisham of his day, the indifferently talented artist whose one genuine inspiration created a genre, and all of a sudden everybody had to have a verismo opera. Of the scores of imitations, only Leoncavallo's *Pagliacci* (1892) came up to the original.

Of the two, I much prefer *Cavalleria* and so will dwell on it here. *Pagliacci's* well-known Prologue and "Laugh, clown, laugh" aria are more instantly recognizable, especially since Caruso made the latter a hit, but I find the

Harlequin-Columbine stage show (the *pagliacci* are a group of traveling players) tiresome and can't wait for Canio, the aggrieved tenor, to off his faithless wife, Nedda, and her wimpy lover, Silvio.

Cavalleria, on the other hand, offers beauties from start to finish. (Amazingly, Mascagni lived long enough to record his opera in 1940 with Gigli in the lead role.) It also provides the enterprising stage director with a magnificent setting—a Sicilian village square, dominated by a church—on which to work his magic. Small wonder that the most musical of movie directors, Francis Ford Coppola, selected the opera as the musical analog and backdrop for the final Corleone tragedy—*The Godfather, Part III.* (The opera is practically a movie score all by itself.) What better counterpoint to an epic of love, death, betrayal, and revenge than an opera about love, death, betrayal, and revenge?

Cav, based on the short story by Giovanni Verga, is something of an odd duck, for during its first ten minutes or so it is less an opera than an orchestral tone poem with offstage voices and, later, a chorus. Far more effectively than Leoncavallo, the twenty-six-year-old Mascagni establishes a sense of time and place through purely musical means. You can almost feel the heat rising from the dusty streets of the remote village, and with the heat of the day comes the heat of the heart, which must find its fullest expression in blood.

As in all great operas, the orchestra is a fully fledged actor in the drama. This is not the orchestra of Wagner, brimming with leitmotifs; nor is it the rum-tum-tiddle-tiddle band of the early Verdi. Imagine the orchestral writing of *Otello* combined with the flexible lyricism of Puccini and you will have some idea of what a miracle Mascagni has wrought. For his particular genius in this opera was not to home in too closely on the lethal love triangle of Turridù, Santuzza, and Alfio, nor on the Turridù-Mamma Lucia relationship. Instead, he draws the whole town into the drama; it's no accident that the first we hear of the main character is his offstage voice. Similarly, the duel between the two men takes place offstage as well. In other words, it's not what happens that's of the highest importance, it's the effect it has on the community. We don't see Turridù being killed by Alfio; instead, the opera's last image is of the scorned and vengeful Santuzza, who has egged on Alfio, collapsing in shock at the news of her lover's death. Fittingly, the last words are sung not by one of the principals but one of the townspeople, who screams that Turridù has been killed.

The highlight, of course, is the illustrious Intermezzo, which arrives two-thirds of the way through the drama as a brief moment of repose before the storm. Santuzza has just informed Alfio that Turridù has been keeping company with Alfio's wife, Lola. What happens next is a foregone conclusion, but just before it does, the stage clears and the Intermezzo sings out. Is there a more perfect three-minute orchestral interlude than this? All aching strings and comforting harps, it sums up not only the hopelessness of Turridù's position, but that of all the villagers. Far from a prettified, irrelevant bit of extraneous lyricism, the Intermezzo is the fulcrum on which the opera turns, and it packs a wallop all out of proportion to its size. Which may be why Coppola chose it to illustrate the lonely death of Michael Corleone.

There's nothing to be ashamed about in liking *Cavalleria rusticana.* It can be a Guilty Pleasure, but it can just as easily, and with total justification, be a Desert Island Disc. I can think of few works in the repertoire to equal it in the freshness of its inspiration; though at first it may seem a conventional Italian romantic opera, that's only because it's so familiar—and in this case familiarity has bred disdain if not contempt. It shouldn't.

Jules Massenet: *Werther.* Another opera in which love must end in death, and a Guilty Pleasure par excellence, is Massenet's masterpiece. For some reason, it has been left to French composers to tackle the masterpieces of German literature: Gounod set Goethe's great poem *Faust,* Part I, while Jules Massenet went for the same author's influential novel *The Sorrows of Young Werther,* which so affected young male readers of the late eighteenth century that a rash of copycat suicides broke out in its wake. ("This book ought to be banned. It's encouraging our young people to blah, blah, blah . . .")

The Germans haven't taken too kindly with this messing with their cultural totems. In Germany, Gounod's *Faust* is sometimes presented as *Marguerite*—just so nobody gets any idea that it does justice to the sacred Goethe. *Werther* ranks a little higher on the evolutionary scale, but the fact remains that, to Germans, Goethe is best left read and unsung, whereas to the French (and the rest of us) he works much better with a little music to deflate his insufferable pomposity and opacity. (Have you ever tried *reading* Part II of *Faust*? I thought not.)

Once again, we have the eternal triangle: Werther is in love with Charlotte (accent the second syllable of both their names), but she is inconveniently engaged, as such women invariably are, to a boring bourgeois clod named Albert (Al-BEAR). Of course, she's crazy about Werther, but the problem is that he's arrived on the scene (old Frankfurt) just a little bit too late; she promised her late mother that she would get hitched to Al, and a promise is a promise, especially when you're a German, even if you're singing in French.

Werther is of course devastated and spends most of the rest of the opera moping around. He bumps into Albert and Charlotte coming out of church one fine September afternoon; Albert, a sport, says, basically, hey, pal, no hard feelings, okay? and suggests that Werther might settle for Charlotte's spunky little fifteen-year-old sister, Sophie, instead. Charlotte appears and hints coyly that maybe they can meet again at Christmas.

In the third act, they do just that. Werther had been writing mad passionate letters to Charlotte, who returns his feelings in spades (well, she has been married for several months): now he shows up at her door, on Christmas Eve. They embrace, but Charlotte breaks away, unable to handle the guilt. Distraught, Werther hurries off, but sends a note to Albert asking to borrow his pistols. Wonder what he means by that . . . ?

The fourth act, which is really the second scene of the third act, finds Werther sprawled on the floor of his study, dying of a gunshot wound. Charlotte, in whose head the light bulb has finally gone off, has rushed to his side, but it's almost too late—almost too late to hear him sing his last aria, that is. Sad songs, they say so much: as Werther dies, Charlotte confesses her love for him—*now* she tells him—and the last words of the opera are "Noël, noël," sung by the oblivious neighborhood children. (*Wozzeck* ends with a similar scene, except that in Berg's opera the kids happily inform Marie's child that its mother's body has just been found.)

Werther is one of the most affecting operas around, and you will never get tired of it. The title role offers the tenor an unending embarrassment of melody, including Werther's great invocation of nature in the first act, and his lovesick outburst that closes the same act; has the sweet agony of infatuation ever been better expressed musically? The opera demands a first-rate lyric tenor in the title role—Alfredo Kraus was masterful—and a sympathetic, attractive soprano as Charlotte. But most of all it requires a conductor who is not afraid to let the agonizing passion of the score shine through. Anyone who has ever felt the desperate pangs of love will find those emotions mirrored in the *Werther* score. More than any other composer, Massenet in this opera captured the pain of impossible and unrequited love—not just once, but again and again, in every note. Werther's suicide seems less a selfish way out than the natural outgrowth of his feelings. His love for Charlotte could not be purer or more intense, and so at the end there is nothing left for him to do except die. What in Goethe seems weak, silly, and self-indulgent becomes, in Massenet's musical analysis, almost heroic. Werther and Charlotte cannot live happily ever after; instead, each is condemned to his and her own private hell, he in death, she in a loveless marriage. There is no happy ending here; in fact, there is not even the possibility of one.

But is that so bad? Our self-indulgent age demands happy endings the way small children do—we find it hard to conceive that lovers should remain apart, or that a silly little abstract concept like wedding vows should prevent a dysfunctional marriage from breaking up, or that one's word might be one's bond, even to (or perhaps especially to) a dead person. But the late eighteenth century was a different time and a different place, and honor mattered. It was unthinkable that Charlotte should run off with Werther; far better for her immortal soul that she suffer in this life, to be rewarded in the next.

Seen this way, the love story between Charlotte and Werther thus becomes a profoundly *moral* tale, not an immoral one. And this is precisely the point I have been trying to make throughout this chapter: that while opera plots may seem to be about a bunch of disreputable outlaws and sexual brigands, they are in fact offered to us as Christian morality plays. An opera about a bunch of saints would not be interesting; it is far more instructive to examine the lives of the least and last among us. Jesus said let him who is without sin cast the first stone, and in opera, no stones fly. But many souls are saved.

Olivier Messiaen: *Saint François d'Assise (Saint Francis of Assisi).* Well, here's an opera about a saint—maybe the saintliest saint of them all. And does it work? You bet it does.

Saint François was premiered on November 28, 1983, in Paris, and I was lucky enough to be present. It is an enormous work, lasting nearly five hours, and scored for huge forces, including a gigantic orchestra and a chorus of 150. Not everyone thought it was wonderful; as we left the house after the first performance, an experienced and respected colleague of mine in the music business remarked that the evening was the most loathsome she had ever spent in the theater.

That was her opinion. Mine is that *Saint François* is a magnificent, dramatically stagnant, probably unperformable, and certainly damned difficult work of genius that we will simply have to live with. (Another such is Ralph Vaughan Williams's *The Pilgrim's Progress.*) Yes, it's more oratorio than opera; yes, it ought to be performed in Chartres Cathedral instead of the Paris Opéra. Yes, it will very likely never enter the repertoire—although it did get a second production in the early nineties at the Salzburg Festival, which is a good sign. But that doesn't mean it isn't wonderful.

Messiaen's particular style is hard to describe, mostly because it is sui generis; nobody else's music sounds anything like his. Part birdsong, part modal, part acerbic modernism, part French lyricism, it is a highly individual synthesis that also derives in part from Messiaen's experience as a church organist. Like his fellow organist Anton Bruckner, Messiaen goes in for massive sonorities that rattle your fundament; the *Turangalîla-Symphonie* is one of the twentieth century's most original symphonic works, and probably the best introduction to Messiaen's mature style.

Still and all, *Saint François* is a masterpiece from start to finish, the opera (he wrote only one) its composer spent all his life working toward. Messiaen, who died in 1992, was a lifelong devout Catholic whose other great passion was the study of birds and birdsong; in *Saint François* he found a natural subject—yes, there is a scene of Saint Francis preaching to the birds—that combined both his enthusiasms.

The plot, if you've read your *Lives of the Saints,* you already know. The work consists simply of eight tableaux, charting the salient stations on Francis's road to salvation. Its highlight is Tableau Five, subtitled "L'ange musicien," or "The Angel of Music." In this blinding bit of musical revelation, a viol-playing angel appears to Francis and reveals unto him a profound vision of the power of music—a vision so strong that Francis says it would have torn the soul from his body had he not fainted dead away. There are few scenes in contemporary opera more powerful, or more beautiful.

But what makes the opera germane to our theme is the second scene, "Lauds," in which Francis realizes that while God made all that is lovely in the world, He has also created all the ugliness. And though Francis may feel revulsion at the horrors and sins of this imperfect world, he must also come to terms with them as part of the natural order. This realization leads in turn to his embrace of the Leper in the next scene—the exact moment when he becomes a saint.

So are we saying, with typical twentieth-century sophistry, that Bad is Good? (It is my contention that the entire history of our century may be viewed as an idiotic attempt to prove that up is down, black is white, and that your mother really didn't know what she was talking about.) Not at all. On the contrary, the point is that it is only by examining evil, by understanding the nature of Wrong—*and embracing it,* the way Francis does the Leper—that we learn about goodness and define for ourselves what is Right. But just as virtue does not exist in the abstract, neither does sin. It is impossible to disprove a negative, so it is only by holding the negative up to the light—of both reason and emotion—that we discover what it is that we really do believe in.

If that philosophy was good enough for Saint Francis, it ought to be good enough for us, too.

• • •

Philip Glass: *Satyagraha.* This is another saintly, philosophical opera, this time on a non-Christian subject. Satyagraha was the name Mohandas Gandhi gave to his political and ethical movement of nonviolent resistance. Contrary to what you may think, Satyagraha was first tried out not in India but in South Africa, where Gandhi spent time before returning to his homeland.

Glass had had a remarkable succès d'estime with his and Robert Wilson's epochal *Einstein on the Beach* in 1976. But after all the fuss over *Einstein* subsided, he was still broke and had to go back to driving a New York City taxicab. For the second installment of what eventually proved to be a trilogy of operas on the subject of great men, Glass worked with a libretto—drawn from the Bhagavad Gita, and sung entirely in Sanskrit—by Constance DeJong and himself that, like the later *Saint François,* is less a narrative than a series of tableaux vivants depicting various scenes from the life.

A bald retelling of the plot would make this opera seem little more than a fashionable concept upon which the composer hung some of his trademark chugga-chugga minimalist music: Gandhi gets outraged over the second-class citizenship afforded to South Africa's large Indian community and organizes a peaceful protest. The end. But it's hardly that simple. Each scene is carefully calibrated and expansively realized; in *Satyagraha,* premiered in Rotterdam in 1980, Glass was already moving away from the strict repetition of his earlier music to a freer, more flexible style that allowed him to reach considerable heights of expression.

To me, *Satyagraha* represents the high-water mark of minimalism. Glass would go on to write another masterpiece, the gloomy *Akhnaten,* a few years later, but the earlier opera is, I believe, superior, if only for the sheer sense of transfigured ecstasy the composer achieves in the remarkable final scene. An illustration of the aftermath of a protest march against discrimination that ended violently, the scene consists of a single musical line for Gandhi—the scale E to E, played on the white keys of the piano—sung slowly and lyrically and repeated over and over and over and over. Nothing could better sum up the budding Mahatma's iron determination coupled with his inner serenity; he has moral force behind his philosophy, before which the British oppression must surely fall, first in South Africa—ever notice how the Brits always seem to tiptoe away from the colonial disasters they leave behind them, and then blame the resulting fiasco on the natives?—and later in India.

Glass has proven to be a remarkably prolific artist, a throwback to the old days when composers (Haydn, for example) didn't sit around waiting for inspiration to conk them on the head, but instead went about their business, writing every day and usually with a specific performance in mind. The once-scorned Glass has become an honored figure on the international operatic scene—something of an elder statesman, even, much to the former hippie and countercultural revolutionary's chagrin. Yet we should honor *Einstein, Satyagraha,* and *Akhnaten* not for their musical politics, but for their stunning beauty.

Each work contains a moment that ranks with anything in opera. The ending of *Einstein,* for example, when one of the speakers intones Samuel M. Johnson's "Two Lovers" text, is heartrendingly gorgeous, an epiphany made all the more concentrated by its position at the end of a very long and challenging work. *Akhnaten,* for its part, contains the pharaoh's radiant "Hymn to the Sun," which is enough to make even the most pagan Egyptian sign up for monotheism on the spot. But the concluding scene of *Satyagraha* has a special place in my heart, as I hope it will in yours.

Piotr Ilyich Tchaikovsky: *Eugene Onegin.* You knew I was going to get to this one eventually. In the first chapter we discussed the piece in the context of how music functions in an operatic context. Now, let's look more carefully at the work itself.

Onegin was not the famed Russian composer's first opera, but it was his first great one. Tchaikovsky was notoriously insecure, and had a habit of destroying pieces that had failed or somehow displeased. His maiden voyage, *The Voyevoda,* ran for only five nights at the Bolshoi in Moscow in 1869, and Tchaikovsky trashed it. (The opera was reconstructed from the parts later.) He also consigned to the flames his next work, *Undine,* which was rejected by the Imperial Opera in St. Petersburg the same year. Material from both works eventually found its way into other scores.

Two more operas preceded *Onegin.* The first, called *The Oprichnik,* was something of a hit, and ran for fourteen performances at the Maryinsky Theater in St. Petersburg, but the composer grew to dislike the piece and refused to revive it after he became famous. The second was *Vakula the Smith,* a comic opera based on Gogol, which was well received, although not well enough to suit Tchaikovsky; he later revised it extensively, and renamed it *The Slippers,* but it never became the success he had hoped for.

But in 1877, two things happened to change Tchaikovsky's life. Out of the blue arrived a passionate letter from a young woman named Antonina Milyukova, who informed the confirmed bachelor that she was madly in love with him; at the same time, a singer suggested Pushkin's novel *Eugene Onegin* as a subject for an opera.

He began by composing the scene that had long been his favorite: Tatiana's passionate epistle to Onegin, in which she confesses her love. In the middle of his labors came another letter from Milyukova, and Tchaikovsky naturally associated the events of his real life with the fictional circumstances of his characters. Determined not to make the same mistake Onegin does, he agreed to meet her and—incredibly—proposed marriage. By late summer, he was making wedding plans and working hard on his opera.

The marriage, of course, was an immediate disaster; Milyukova was an immature and unstable woman and Tchaikovsky was an inveterate homosexual. By October the composer had already attempted suicide, and fled to the home of his brother, Anatoli, who took him abroad to recover. This brief taste of marital bliss was enough to knock Tchaikovsky off his compositional stride, and the opera was not ready for performance until March of 1879. Tchaikovsky's intention was that it should be performed by conservatory students, and it was not until 1884 that *Onegin* got a big-league production in St. Petersburg. That was all it needed, and it quickly became the most popular and beloved of all Russian operas.

And with good reason. *Onegin* has everything going for it. Begin with Pushkin's story, a case study in pigheadedness that has universal resonance. How many of us, faced with the opportunity of a deep and satisfying relationship, pass up the chance, only to rue the day weeks, months, or even years later? The plot has some similarity to *Werther* except that Onegin's fate is far crueler: Tatiana may be condemned to a loveless marriage, but Onegin does not take the easy way out as Werther did; instead, the haughty man is humbled by the blinding realization of what a fool he has been, and must live out the rest of his days with that knowledge staring him in the face every time he looks in the mirror.

Then there is the music. Tell Tchaikovsky the news: it is customary to dismiss him as a second-tier composer who relies primarily on pretty tunes and flashy orchestration. But I defy anyone to show me why *Onegin* is not one of opera's most psychologically penetrating and emotionally affecting works. The Letter Scene, Lensky's pathetic aria before his duel with Onegin, the rousing polonaise, and even Prince Gremin's last-act aria, in which he, all unawares, tells Onegin how much happiness Tatiana has brought him—all these moments add up to an overwhelming operatic experience, one that never fails to move us because it so profoundly humanistic.

Tchaikovsky may not have been physically able to appreciate heterosexual love, although he tried, but he was certainly able to convey it through musical means. There is not a cardboard character in the opera—not Olga, Tatiana's airhead sister; not Lensky, whose aria in the first act is a model of youthful passion; and not even Gremin, who could have been merely a Russian version of Massenet's old-fart Albert. The composer took each one seriously and lavished his most beautiful music on them all. There are no deviates here, no home wreckers, no homicidal maniacs or suicidal basket cases. Just real people, caught up in real emotions, hampered by a iron caste system, but not crushed by it. Instead, they are done in by their own stubborn pride. And what could be more natural than that?

Giacomo Puccini: *La bohème, Tosca,* and *La rondine.* Another composer whose reputation has suffered at the hands of his popularity is Giacomo Puccini, who more or less closed the book on the era of the classic Italian opera. Puccini is a crowd pleaser, and thus easily attacked for being a panderer of cheap, meretricious sentiment, but such criticism seems to me profoundly wrong, and certainly demeans Puccini's indisputable accomplishment as a vocal-music composer and orchestrator.

A problem with Puccini is that his operas are so popular they practically define the term *opera* itself, at least in the public mind. Few opera companies can manage a season without at least one Puccini staple, for the simple reason that they are as good, and as beloved, as advertised. Oscar Wilde said it would take a heart of stone not to laugh at the death of Little Nell, and I suppose the sophisticates can say the same of the death of Mimi in *La bohème* as well. But so what? The scene sends chills up and down the spine every time.

And don't think Puccini didn't know it. Few composers

were as careful to calibrate their effects as Puccini; in his operas, nothing is left to chance. He had a keen eye for the suitable subject—even when, as in the case of David Belasco's English-language play *Madame Butterfly,* he could barely understand a word of it—and knew exactly how to get his librettists Giuseppe Giacosa and Luigi Illica to whip the material into operatic shape.

One of the most remarkable things about Puccini, and a quality that is often overlooked, is the consistently high level of his inspiration. Unlike, say, Verdi, he did not begin his career with a string of duds or lesser works. As with Richard Strauss, there were two false starts, *Le villi* (which is an opera, literally, about the willies) and *Edgar,* and then—bang! *Manon Lescaut.* After which followed *Bohème, Tosca, Madama Butterfly, La fanciulla del West* (*The Girl of the Golden West*), *La rondine* (*The Swallow*), *Il trittico* (three one-act operas, including *Il tabarro, Suor Angelica,* and *Gianni Schicchi*), and, finally, *Turandot.* That's an amazing percentage of winners that few other opera composers can match.

I guess what I'm saying is that one of the things I admire most about old Giacomo is his professionalism. Opera composition in our time has become the province of amateurs and first-timers, composers who labor mightily on their masterpieces, then drop the scores on conductors' desks and in performers' laps and say: just do it. No matter that their lack of experience may necessitate revisions, the fixing of unsingable passages and impossible high or low notes, the adjustment of some orchestrational faux pas that interferes with the vocal line. Puccini, however, was a man of the theater down to his toenails.

The three operas I've singled out should just be the beginning. Once you've discovered mature Puccini, I guarantee that you will like nearly everything else he wrote, with the possible exception of *La fanciulla del West* and the middle installment of the trilogy, *Suor Angelica,* although both have lovely moments.

But nobody doesn't like *La bohème,* the opera for lovers everywhere. (Remember the movie *Moonstruck*?) Puccini's freshest and happiest music suffuses the score, and each scene is practically its own highlight film: Rodolfo and Mimi, falling in love while searching for her key on the floor of his freezing garret; the bohemians on the town in Act II, reveling to the strains of Musetta's Waltz; the inevitable reality check of Act III; and Mimi's death of consumption in Act IV. Every note is a joy, every emotion one that is familiar to each member of the audience. Rodolfo and Mimi, Marcello and Musetta, and the rest of the gang may be, when considered in the cold light of day, a bunch of silly, self-indulgent poseurs, eternal graduate students who really ought to grow up and get a life. But they are also our friends.

Tosca, on the other hand, is high drama—Sardooodledum, as Shaw called it, punning on the name of the playwright Victorien Sardou, whose play *La Tosca* forms the basis of the libretto. Tosca is a fiery opera singer; her lover Cavaradossi is a firebrand revolutionary; her tormentor Scarpia is the fire-breathing chief of the secret police. From the beginning, the emotions of *Tosca* are pitched high, and the opera features one coup de théâtre after another. The first act ends with a magnificent procession in the church of Sant' Andrea della Valle; Act II contains Tosca's dramatic murder of the lecherous Scarpia and her famous aria, "Vissi d'arte"; while Act III has the opera's most beloved tune, "E lucevan le stelle." From start to finish, the action moves swiftly toward its appointed tragic conclusion, and we love every minute of it.

La rondine (say La RON-dee-nay) may be lesser Puccini, but it contains some of his most ravishing music, and I cannot understand why it is not programmed more often. Perhaps the opera's checkered history is partly to blame—it had the bad fortune to be scheduled at the same time as World War I—but more likely it is the clumsy libretto, which is a kind of *La traviata* Lite. Still, I urge you to get to know it. The central character of Magda is given one gorgeous tune after another, and overall Puccini displays a deftness and understatement that is largely absent from his other works.

Whichever Puccini you fall in love with (and you will fall in love), please keep in mind that what you're reacting to, once again, is the humanity of the characters. Even the flamboyant Tosca touches us; she seems a bitch right up to "Vissi d'arte," but in the aria, in which she explains how she lives her life and why, she reaches out and touches us, a larger-than-life woman in a heap of trouble who is no less real than any of us, watching her from the safety of our seats.

Wolfgang Amadeus Mozart: *The Marriage of Figaro; Così fan tutte; Don Giovanni; The Magic Flute.* Which brings us to the greatest humanist of them all, Wolfgang Amadé (he never signed himself "Amadeus") Mozart. I have chosen his four best-known operas to talk about here, but please take this merely as the beginning of what should be a lifelong investigation, on your part, of all his musical-theater works, from the youthful *Il sogno di Scipione* to the last opera, *La clemenza di Tito.*

Each of the four universally acknowledged masterpieces—the first three with Italian librettos by Lorenzo Da Ponte, the fourth a German-language singspiel—has won a permanent place in the repertoire. In a sense, the modern opera hit list begins with Mozart since few of Handel's many operas are staged today, except by specialty companies, and Haydn, for all his manifest accomplishment as a symphonist, was not able to bring the same level of inspiration to his operas.

Why not? It's a good question. Mozart admired Papa Haydn above all other composers, a feeling richly reciprocated by the much older Haydn, who in a letter to Mozart's real papa, the formidable Leopold Mozart, wrote of Wolfgang that "Before God and as an honest man I tell you that your son is the greatest composer known to me." Few musicians would care to choose between Haydn's 104 and Mozart's 41 symphonies, and the chamber music of each composer, particularly the string quartets, exists on a similarly exalted level of inspiration.

And yet, the operas . . . The authoritative *Complete Opera Book* by Gustav Kobbé deems not a single Haydn opera worthy of inclusion in its 1,400 pages. And yet Haydn wrote many operas—twenty-one between the years 1762 and 1783 alone—and operatic composition dominated his life from 1776 to 1790. Haydn thought very highly of his operas, many of which were composed for the court theater at Esterháza, his prince's rural retreat. But he could be more than a little defensive about them: "I assure you that no such work has been heard in Paris up to now, nor perhaps in Vienna; my misfortune is that I live in the country," he wrote to his publisher in 1781 about his latest work. Few others felt the same way, however, and by 1787 Haydn was gradually coming to the conclusion that it was pointless to compete with Mozart. Offered a commission to write an opera for Prague, he turned it down, observing that "no man can brook comparison with the great Mozart."

On the surface, there is not a great deal of difference between the musical styles of the two men. So what is it that separates them? Why so wide a gulf between the achievement of Mozart and Haydn? The answer is simple: Mozart's characters are real people.

We keep coming back to this, but it's worth repeating because humanism is the key to understanding and loving opera. *Opera must be about real people, with real emotions we all can share.* Haydn's operas such as *Il mondo della luna* (it used to be translated as *The Man in the Moon* but a better rendering is *The World of the Moon*), *Armida,* and *L'isola disabitata (The Desert Island)* have many lovely musical passages, but they remain just that—musical passages without dramatic substance or significance.

Mozart, on the other hand, is nothing but substance. From the first masterpiece, *Idomeneo,* to the mature works of his last years (remember, he died a month short of his thirty-sixth birthday), Mozart is first to last a composer of overwhelming humanity. There are no abstractions in the mature Mozart, no cardboard characters that stand in for lofty philosophical ideals. There are only breathing, sweating, fighting, loving human beings, living their lives in the best way they know how, sometimes succeeding, sometimes failing, but always trying.

In *Figaro* we have a stock situation: the Count wants to sleep with the serving girl Susanna on the night of her wedding to his valet, Figaro, and he must be outwitted. Mozart turns this Beaumarchais bedroom farce into a work of deep sympathy for all the players—not just Figaro and Susanna, but for the lusty page boy, Cherubino, and, most of all, for the regal Countess (who turns up as Rosina in Rossini's "prequel," *The Barber of Seville),* whose magnanimity closes the opera on a note of forgiveness and love.

Don Giovanni, considered by many to be the greatest opera ever written, presents the familiar rakehell for our inspection, and a very bad fellow he is indeed. As the opera opens, he is attempting to rape Donna Anna; discovered by her father, the Commendatore, the Don challenges the older man to a duel and kills him. It is this sin, not his relentless, compulsive conquest of women (documented so brilliantly in Leporello's "Catalogue" aria), that eventually condemns him to hellfire and damnation. Date-rape activists are going to hate this opera: Donna Anna, his putative "victim," seems attracted to the Don, while the seduced-and-abandoned Donna Elvira is obviously crazy about him. Zerlina, the peasant girl, goes off with him willingly. There's something about a man in a codpiece . . .

The funny part is, the Don strikes out with every one of them, a point the feminists will probably ignore. He is interrupted in his conquest of Anna, Elvira is an old flame he cannot quite rekindle, and Zerlina is rescued by her boyfriend, Masetto. The Don is strangely impotent for such a stud; in the end it is the murder—in fact, it is the murder victim—that comes back to haunt him. When Giovanni rashly invites the statue of the Commendatore, which stands over the grave of the dead man, to dinner, it accepts. The penultimate scene, so chillingly forecast musically by the magnificent overture, shows the Don refusing to renounce his lascivious ways; if he must go to Hell, at least he's going to go as a standup guy.

Nowadays, of course, the Don would either cop a plea or mount an aggressive victimization defense. He had an abused childhood; he had a repressed memory; his grandma wouldn't bake him his favorite cookies. Maybe he would blame it all on Leporello, or on the women. He would probably have to do some time, of course, but if he went before the Kultur Nazi tribunal, confessed that he was a sex addict and promised to sin no more, a book deal and an appearance on *Donahue* would be waiting for him on the other side. And you know what? Women would throw themselves at him.

PC types beware: *Così fan tutte* is just as likely to frost you as *Don Giovanni.* Even the title is guaranteed to get your goat: it means, roughly translated, "That's the way all women are," or, "What do you expect from a broad, anyway?" In this opera, the women are bona fide sex objects. An old roué named Don Alfonso wagers a couple of wet-behind-the-ear swains named Ferrando and Guglielmo that their girlfriends, the sisters Fiordiligi and Dorabella, would be unfaithful to them should they ever let them out of their sight. Oh, yeah? say the boys. Yeah! says Don Alfonso, who enlists the saucy little serving wench Despina (female characters in Mozart whose names end in "ina" must invariably be described as saucy) to help him prove his point.

The boys march off, allegedly to war; the girls are heartbroken. The boys march back, disguised as "Albanians," and each promptly sets out to woo the other's lady. Ferrando heads for Fiordiligi (tenor and soprano) and Guglielmo for Dorabella (baritone and mezzo). Although the savvy opera fan can deduce from the vocal categories that these are the correct pairings, the remainder of the opera focuses on how the new couples fall in love. At the end, the cruel jest is revealed, and the lovers are supposed to return to their original betrotheds. But we wonder. . . .

It's a cold, calculating, and very schematic (and very eighteenth century, for that matter) libretto that Da Ponte concocted—far better literarily than the untidy *Don Giovanni,* where it's clear the poet ran out of ideas for Act II—but once again Mozart humanizes it with his music. *Così* is no rationalist tract, but a richly nuanced road map of the human heart; while the words may be cynical, the music is definitely not, and in many ways I prefer it to all other Mozart operas. The six characters (there aren't any others, just a small chorus) are each painstakingly individualized, and by the opera's end there can be no question that Ferrando and Fiordiligi really have fallen in love. Dorabella capitulates much earlier than her sister, and her freshly minted relationship with Guglielmo seems less secure. But having watched Fiordiligi struggling to choose between fidelity and nascent love, we believe her emotions are deeper and more genuine.

The ending of *Così* is one of opera's great and-then-what-happens? Surely, we say, these couples can't pretend the last three hours never occurred. Surely, they can't be expected to fulfill their prior engagements. But what if they are part of a society that prizes duty over temptation, that eschews an if-it-feels-good-then-do-it ethos in favor of a more stable social philosophy? The close of *Così* is ambiguous, and probably in a way that Mozart and Da Ponte, who could not have foreseen the sexual revolution or the Playboy Philosophy, would never have imagined. This, too, is part of the work's afterlife, and we will continue to debate it as long as opera houses are still around.

The last of the quartet, *The Magic Flute,* stands apart from its siblings not only by virtue of its language but by its intention. *Flute* was written for the popular theater, not the opera house: think of it as a kind of off-off-off-Broadway show. Mozart was frankly trying to write a crowd pleaser, and, in the few weeks of life he had left after the premiere, it tickled him no end that he succeeded.

The libretto was by one Emanuel Schikaneder, a singer, playwright, composer, and producer who had played Hamlet and arrogated the role of Papageno in *Flute* for himself. Like Mozart, Schikaneder was a Mason, and the naïve-mystical libretto is rife with Masonic symbolism. Once again, this is an opera calculated to outrage feminists: the women, led by the Queen of the Night, are the bad guys, while the men, whose leader is Sarastro, are good. Of course, it takes the hero Tamino a while to figure this out, since it is the Queen who enlists him on his quest to find and rescue her lovely daughter Pamina from Sarastro's putative clutches.

Even with a cartoon story like this, Mozart could not resist humanizing it. The Caliban-like birdman Papageno and his mate Papagena represent the common people, while Tamino (a Japanese prince) and Pamina stand for the nobility. Sarastro and the Queen of the Night, of course, are the higher (or lower) powers. And yet Mozart poured out his heart in his music: the poignant duet for Pamina and Papageno that celebrates the love of man and woman; the Papageno-Papagena duet at the opera's close, a hymn to the joys of procreation; Tamino's "Portrait" aria, in which he glimpses Pamina's beauty in a cameo and immediately falls in love. Despite the heavy symbolism of the story, the characters are never archetypes.

If it seems that I am emphasizing Mozart's humanism, I am. The eighteenth century was a periwigged and peruked era, but it was also the wellspring of all the civil liberties we hold dear today: a profound understanding of the nature of love, a sympathy for mankind's foibles, a desire for political freedom (the hidden agenda of *The Marriage of Figaro*), a recognition of the rights o' man. What does our allegedly enlightened century have to offer besides these virtues? Fascism, Nazism, and communism all posited the essential worthlessness of the individual; psychiatry, at least the way it has been perverted by the legal system, seeks to absolve the individual from responsibility for his or her actions; the twelve-tone system, which seemed as invulnerable as communism until its collapse in the late 1970s, sought to remove inspiration as the operative principle of composition and replace it with a schematic intellectuality that appealed to almost no one.

This is why Mozart still speaks so strongly and clearly to us. He is every bit as revolutionary today as he was two hundred years ago. Nay, more so, for it is not too hard to imagine some politically correct cretin or moral-majority moron raising objections to the content of Mozart's operas—don't laugh, they've already attacked *Show Boat* and *Peter Pan*. Mozart's operas are declarations of independence—independence from cant, hypocrisy, and conformism. They should be treasured not only for their musical content but for what they tell us about ourselves.

Richard Wagner: *Der Ring des Nibelungen; Tristan und Isolde; Die Meistersinger von Nürnberg*. And so we come to an end of our little survey, and what better way to conclude than with the Wizard of Bayreuth, the most influential composer of the nineteenth century and, it might be argued, of all time?

Wagner is such a mighty phenomenon that we can only touch on a few salient issues in this short discussion. It has been said that more has been written about Wagner than about anyone else with the exception of Napoleon Bonaparte and Jesus Christ; that's how important Wagner was, and is. But we're not interested here in Wagner's credentials. Instead, we're trying to understand exactly why we're expected to sit through the four-day-long *Ring* cycle—*Das*

Rheingold, Die Walküre, Siegfried, and *Götterdämmerung*—or why the five-hour music dramas of *Tristan* and *Meistersinger* are worth our time.

If there's one thing most of us don't have these days, it's time. Wagner, however, will transport you to a timeless world you didn't even know existed. Hell, *he* probably didn't even know it existed, except in his unspoken subconscious. For if you thought Puccini & Co. reeked of primitive emotions, then what will you make of Wagner? Beyond the incestuous relationships of the *Ring,* beyond the illicit love affair of Tristan and Isolde, beyond all the various other couplings that lie at the root of Wagner, there is a fundamental sense of sex and sexuality that pervades all of Wagner's music. More than any other opera composer, Wagner communicates directly with our deepest natures.

And that's why he's such a fascinating fellow. Unlovable in real life—to the usual tiresome catalogue of marital infidelity and habitual impecuniousness you can add slavish sycophancy to anyone he thought could finance his projects (such as Bavaria's famous Mad King Ludwig, who made Wagner his personal guru) and, in general, a feeling that the world owed him a living—Wagner was nevertheless a genius who created a universe and invited to us become a part of it.

In the *Ring,* Wagner attempted nothing less than a grand musico-philosophical synthesis of the known universe and essentially pulled it off. The *Ring* has offered endless food for thought from its first performance as a cycle in Bayreuth in 1876—Shaw, for example, saw it as a socialist commentary on the evils of capitalism—and a new *Ring* production is an automatic highlight of any opera season. In tracing the story of Wotan's fateful bargain for the Rhinegold and the Ring that was fashioned from it Wagner created a metaphor for society and social disintegration that is even more potent today than it was a century ago.

How potent? Let me tell you about the most impressive

audience reaction I have ever heard. It came during the production of Wagner's *Der Ring des Nibelungen* in Bayreuth in 1983. Bayreuth is the small city in northern Bavaria where the great composer founded and built his own theater, and to this day the local populace retains a proprietary interest in matters Wagnerian. That year, the artistic team included conductor Georg Solti and director Peter Hall, both knights of whatever's left of the British Empire. Anticipation was high, not because of Hall particularly, but because of Solti, whose groundbreaking complete *Ring* on records in the late fifties and early sixties made phonographic history.

For various reasons, however, the production was a fiasco. For one thing, the weather was unbearably hot (over 100 degrees Fahrenheit) in a country manifestly devoid of air conditioning, or even fans, and conditions inside the Festspielhaus during the four performances of opening week were almost intolerable. Gentlemen doffed their nearly obligatory tuxedo jackets and sat sweltering in shirtsleeves; the ladies, meanwhile, quickly abandoned the brocade evening gowns they wore on the first night, and started showing up in what appeared to be their nighties and their underwear. It was quite a sight.

Artistically, matters were even worse. Sir Georg and Lady Solti seemed to go out of their way to annoy the locals with what was widely viewed as their fancy-pants ways, and the Bayreuth Orchestra, one of the finest in the world, frankly sabotaged the conductor in retaliation, delivering one of its technically poorest performances in memory (in music it can play in its sleep).

Worst of all, though, was Hall's contribution, a badly conceived and hideously executed production that was neither avant-garde nor traditional but simply inept. Aside from one delightful touch, the Rhinemaidens frolicking stark naked in the water as *Das Rheingold* opened—envied by one and all in the sweltering audience—the conception was an arrogant disaster, and sitting through it was the severest test of patience I have ever experienced in any theater.

By the end of the week (the *Ring* consists of three full-length, i.e., incredibly long, operas plus a Prelude which runs more than two hours all by itself) it was payback time. The cast was cheered for its forbearance, and Solti was received tepidly. Then everyone waited to see whether Hall and his production partner, William Dudley, would emerge for their solo bow. They did not. When they finally did appear, they were surrounded for protection by Solti and the entire cast. Nevertheless, the audience found them and, almost as one, roared its disapproval. The demonstration went on for several minutes, to be repeated when Hall and Dudley finally summoned up the courage for a joint bow. Never was booing more richly deserved.

(Naturally, the chauvinistic British press didn't see it quite that way. Noting that many of the production principals were British, either by birth or adoption, the lickspittle minions of Fleet Street all week had been proclaiming the "English *Ring*" as a great day for England.)

So you see that folks take opera seriously. In Bayreuth's case, the reaction sprang from a deep and abiding knowledge of Wagner. It was not that the audience was resistant to change or reinterpretation: Wolfgang Wagner, the festival's director, is the composer's grandson (of a man born in 1813!) and, together with his more creative brother Wieland, he led the Wagner Festival out of its post-Hitler ashes and into the twentieth century. The Hall *Ring* was quickly scrapped in favor of a new production by the German director Harry Kupfer, whose view of the piece was far more ambitious, outrageous, and intellectually challenging than Hall's. It met with some token resistance at first (more pro forma than anything, I suspect) but quickly won over critics and civilians alike through the sheer dramatic power of the director's vision.

The enormous effort in composing the *Ring* demanded

some surcease, and so, between Acts II and III of *Siegfried,* Wagner took a break and wrote *Tristan* and *Meistersinger,* two complementary works. *Tristan* is highly chromatic; *Meistersinger* is diatonic. *Tristan* is an illustration of the intimate relationship between Eros and Thanatos; *Meistersinger* dwells on the vitality of young love, and how age must make way for youth and beauty.

In his works, Wagner does more than humanize his characters: he makes us humanize them. Wagner was a consummate man of the theater, but once you enter his enchanted world the proscenium arch disappears and you are sucked into the vortex. Tristan, Eva, Walther, Siegfried et alia are not characters anymore, they are more real than you are, and you exist in their world at their sufferance. So watch your step.

In the great Act II love duet from *Tristan,* for example, we are made to feel as much an intruder on an incredibly intimate love scene as King Mark and the rest of the troops when they come crashing in; the music practically screams at us to get out. The finale of *Meistersinger,* a pageant in which the medieval town of Nuremberg turns out for the great song contest, brings to life the Middle Ages in a way that mere literature or even painting cannot. *This* is how those people feel, we think, as if we were somehow inside their skins.

What Wagner does, in essence, is to put us on the stage along with his principals. No other composer can make this claim, which is why no other composer can touch Wagner in the power of his music or in its effect on the psyche. Wagner is that most dangerous of artists, the subversive who is able to defy any form of censorship because he has eliminated the middle man and taken his argument directly to the hearts and minds of the listeners. "Here time and space are one" remarks Gurnemanz in *Parsifal,* and the same may be said for all of Wagner's great works. They exist on a separate plane, in a parallel universe, and we privileged few are given entry, through some kind of musical warp drive, and allowed to stay awhile. After a performance of Wagner we may leave the theater and go home, but the theater will not leave us.

And there you have it—a basic repertoire that you can be proud to share with family and friends. Obviously, there are many, many other operas that you will want to get to know, and over the course of time, you will. Who knows, someday you may even want to add *Rinaldo* and *Norma* to the list, which is fine with me.

But this selection has been designed to do two things. The first is to give you an overview of operatic history, as well as an appreciation of its fundamental unity. From the time of Monteverdi to our own day, *plus ça change* has been the byword; the same moral and spiritual issues that occupied the earliest opera composers continue to obsess contemporary artists and are reflected in their work. The common thread running through all the choices has been how the characters deal with the extreme psychological, emotional, and physical states into which their creators have plunged them, and what meanings we, the audience, can derive from their experiences.

The second purpose has been to provide you with the building blocks for the creation of your own, personalized basic repertoire. In opera, as in so much of life, there is no one right way to do things; instead, the art form admits of many possibilities, and while I personally may have rejected some of them (and, in these pages, I have), you are free to do what you like. So go ahead: charge into baroque or bel canto; become a vocal nut or an old-recording freak; fixate on the life and times of a single singer and become an expert. Become an opera nut, for that matter. Be my guest.

Just don't blame me when it happens.

Chapter 6

What About Broadway?, or Does It Have to Be Funny and Foreign?

Popular songs are those written, published and sung, whistled and hummed by the great American unmusical public, as distinguished from the more highly cultivated class which often decries and scoffs at the tantalizing and ear-haunting melodies that are heard from ocean to ocean in every shape and form.

—CHAS. K. HARRIS, COMPOSER OF "AFTER THE BALL"

I just have to jump around when I sing. But it ain't vulgar. It's just the way I feel. I don't feel sexy when I'm singin'. If that was true, I'd be in some kind of institution and some kind of sex maniac.

—ELVIS PRESLEY

We're more popular than Jesus now.

—JOHN LENNON

What you probably didn't realize, before you started this book, is that you already know a lot more about opera than you thought you did. Anyone who has ever seen *Show Boat, The King and I,* or *Carousel* has seen a form of opera; anyone who has ever enjoyed *The Merry Widow* or *The Student Prince* has come within striking distance of one. Is pop music more to your taste? Then what do you think *Tommy, Quadrophenia, Jesus Christ Superstar,* and *Evita* are? And *Sweeney Todd* and *Into the Woods*? That's right: the O word.

This assertion never fails to stir controversy. I've already briefly considered Sondheim and Webber, the two leading exponents of what used to be called musical comedy in the late twentieth century, who for some reason are forever being pitted against one another by their advocates as if Broadway weren't big enough for both of them. Is not! Is so! Is not! Is so! On such a level does the argument rage. But let's look more closely.

Andrew Lloyd Webber and Tim Rice's first show was a fifteen-minute children's musical called *Joseph and the Amazing Technicolor Dreamcoat.* A success almost from the first—especially when a London critic named Derek Jewell "discovered" the work in the pages of his newspaper—the little show has grown and grown over the years until it has last achieved its true, elephantine, Webberian incarnation in the Broadway productions of the eighties and nineties. Their next effort, called an opera from the beginning, was *Superstar,* followed by another opera, *Evita,* the third and final Lloyd Webber–Rice show. The audacity of the boys! To arrogantly invite comparison of their humble works with the very greatest of Verdi, Puccini et alia! Or so some of the critics wrote. And so many of the critics still think.

They think so because they are determined to maintain the almost entirely fictional split between high and low culture to which they have dedicated their lives. Sad to say, newspapers and magazines across America have subscribed to this fallacy, with the result that many of the most important new musical works get reviewed by drama critics who don't have the slightest notion about the function of music on the stage (why do you think they call it "musical comedy"?) and insist on treating even the most through-composed musical (in which nearly every word is sung) as a kind of play that, unaccountably, has music going on all the time. And so we are presented with the sorry spectacle of Sondheim and Webber shows being discussed in the pages of the *New York Times* as if they were more akin to the plays of Eugene O'Neill or Athol Fugard than *The Magic Flute* and *Carmen* (each of which contains far more spoken dialogue than *The Phantom of the Opera*).

In other words, it's a silly and arbitrary distinction, and it would simply be amusing were it not so deleterious to the health of the art form. In New York City, it is a popular sport to speculate on the reasons for the dearth of new musicals—or, indeed, the dearth of new anything—on Broadway. Economics, unions, the Times Square (yes, that *Times* Square) neighborhood—all are routinely blamed. Without ascribing too much power to the drama critic of the *Times,* I would like to suggest that if you were a composer, you too might be discouraged at the prospect of having your biggest and most important work reviewed by someone to whom the very presence of your score is either irrelevant or downright annoying.

The matter becomes even more ridiculous when you consider that once a Broadway show reaches a certain age, it often turns up a mile north, at the New York State Theater in Lincoln Center, where the New York City

Opera annually presents classic musicals. *Then* the music critics troop out and weigh in, two or three decades too late to make any difference.

Whence comes this foolish cultural division? From the time of the Minnesingers, there has always been high and low culture, apportioned along class lines. But composers certainly felt free to help themselves to material from both worlds. The multiplicity of Renaissance masses bearing the title *L'Homme armé* (*The Armed Man*) is a direct result of the incredible popularity of a vulgar song of the period, which even the highest-falutin' composers managed to work into their carefully wrought contrapuntal homages to God. A rough equivalent today might be an outbreak of symphonies on the tune of the Beatles' *Eleanor Rigby;* think of the howls that would bring.

Howls from the classical critics, that is; they (we?) are often their (our?) own worst enemies. For one of the reasons the whole classical music establishment has worked itself into such a pickle in the postwar period is the reluctance of many of the tribe to admit that the cozy little culture gulch of the 1950s is gone forever. In the vulgar, mean-spirited land of Roseanne, there's no longer any room at the inn for *Amahl and the Night Visitors.* Laugh, clown, laugh at the spectacle of Pavarotti waving his hanky at a stadium full of howling drunkards, but in one sense the national and international culture has reverted to its early twentieth-century form, when Caruso was a celebrity pitchman and John McCormack became a zillionaire by singing treacly encores like "The Rose of Tralee."

So do I think that much of today's pop music can also qualify as art? Yes I do. I also believe that the best and the brightest examples of the Broadway show also qualify as opera, by whatever standard you choose to use. I even think that a show that was both a West End and Broadway *failure* qualifies as an opera, so if you will please bear with me, students, we will now parse the best darn flop that ever crashed and burned on the Great White Way. I refer, of course, to the Tim Rice–Boys of ABBA masterpiece, *Chess.*

Originally issued as a double album (remember those?) in 1984, the show was the brainchild of Rice, who had broken off with Lloyd Webber some years before, and Benny Andersson and Björn Ulvaeus, the male half of the quintessentially seventies Swedish megagroup. It hardly seemed promising. ABBA was widely regarded as Eurobubblegum, admittedly infectious but utterly devoid of content (certainly in comparison with the recently deceased, and immediately sainted, Beatles). Several years before, Rice had seen his lyrics for the song "Memory" turned down in favor of ones by director Trevor Nunn, ending his relationship with Lloyd Webber in a burst of acrimony, and many thought that without his songwriting partner he would fade from view.

Chess was Rice's counterattack, his attempt to show that he could still have a hit without Lloyd Webber. The story was a cold war–era parable of two chess players, one American and one Russian, and their struggle not only for chess supremacy but for the love of the same woman, a Hungarian refugee named Florence. The ins and outs of the plot are not important, except insofar as they gave Rice a chance to comment poetically on circumstances that closely mirrored his own complicated love life: the Russian is not only the object of Florence's affection but also that of his long-suffering wife, and in a duet remarkable for its poignant symphany, "I Know Him So Well," both women sing of the impossibility of either of them ever making him happy. It was no secret that Rice was having an open affair with *Chess*'s (and *Evita*'s) leading lady, Elaine Paige, while still very much married to his long-suffering wife, Jane. *Chess,* then, was not only Rice's bid for commercial success without Lloyd Webber, it was a glimpse into his own complicated, cynical, but still deeply humanistic psyche.

As luck would have it, though, *Chess* came to the stage

in the same London season as *The Phantom of the Opera,* which wiped it out. From the outset, the show was dogged by bad fortune, including the illness and death of its director, Michael Bennett, just before the London opening. The omnipresent Trevor Nunn took over, maintaining Bennett's you-are-there, media-rich conception in London but changing the show dramatically for its New York incarnation (new sets, new characters, new songs, new book, lots of new dialogue). Neither production adequately captured the show's emotional center, and the Broadway version was widely panned. It opened and closed within a couple of months in 1988, and that was the end of *Chess* in the bright lights of the cruel big city.

A few months later I was visiting with Rice at his former country home near Cambridge and we got to talking about *Chess.* He admitted its flaws on the stage—flaws that may have been insuperable—but offered this epitaph: "It was a great album, though."

And so it is—from its first Rodgers-and-Hammersteinian chorus to the last note of the final anthem, *Chess* is a brilliant achievement that will only grow in stature with the passing of the years. (Remember, you read it here first.) Its quotidian flaws, including the inadvertent competition with the *Phantom* steamroller and the unfortunate coincidence of Mikhail Gorbachev's perestroika movement, which removed the Soviet Bogeyman from common parlance, will be forgotten in favor of its memorable melodies, its clever construction, its dazzling eclecticism (Benny and Björn's range of styles is even wider and more accomplished than Webber's in *Phantom*), and Rice's bittersweet lyrics, all of which contribute to one of the most important scores of the eighties, a decade notable for its operatic/music-theater triumphs.

The show opens with the deceptively cheerful "Merano," a wry ode to the joys of tourist fleecing in the picturesque South Tyrolean town that wound up in Italy after World War I. Rock score, my foot: the very first notes are played on the flute, soon accompanied by the horn. "Is this *The Sound of Music?* " asks the first stage direction. "Tyrolean hats, leather pants, yodels and dancing. Snow-capped mountain peaks and icy rivers. Grapes and the benefits of the spa."

The music, for chorus and orchestra, continues along its merry path until the arrival of the American, whose bumptious drums and heavy guitar-lick entrance is one of the most striking on record. "It's East-West, and the money's sky-high," he sings.

The Russian watches his opponent on television; his advisers try to convince him the American is Bobby Fischer-crazy, but he knows better: crazy like fox! He dismisses his handler, Molokov, in a bitter duet, and muses on his chosen profession: "Who needs a dream? Who needs ambition? Who'd be the fool in my position?" he sings in "Where I Want to Be."

The tournament opens with the Arbiter's caustic "The Opening Ceremony" number. "This is not the start of World War Three," he sings, "no political ploys/I think both your constitutions are terrific so/Now you know—be good boys." It continues as a chorus of Merchandisers plug their chess match spinoffs, hawking their T-shirts and chess sets with a callous verve that was farfetched in 1984 but which in our day of the disgusting "I'm going to Disney World" commercialism that has infected even the Olympics seems if anything underimagined.

The quartet that follows, "A Model of Decorum and Tranquillity," is one of the show's most elegant and intricate numbers, put together with an astonishing sophistication by the composers. The two camps argue over every conceivable aspect of the match, including where the wood for the chessboard should come from. Back at the hotel, the American's assistant, Florence, berates him for his boorish behavior ("You want to lose your only friend?"). She then delivers herself of one of *Chess*'s showstoppers, the unabashedly derisive aria "Nobody's Side," in which she vents her pessimistic philosophy that no one is to be trusted, ever. "Everybody's playing the game/But nobody's rules are the same/Nobody's on nobody's side."

This song, sung by Paige on the record, sums up the sardonic spirit of *Chess,* and perhaps accounts for its failure. Who can love an opera in which each of the characters is a scheming, selfish son of a bitch? (Well, you loved *Evita,* didn't you?) And yet the song is so potent, so full of defiant angst, that it makes the fabulous Florence an irresistible figure, a lonely woman who can never make a promise or a plan, and takes a little love where she can.

The first game is a silent-movie affair, told orchestrally in the eponymous number "Chess," in which themes heard earlier in the show are combined and intertwined so that we can easily follow not only the match but the emotional resonance behind it. It is no surprise, therefore, that the next number finds Florence and the Russian meeting in a private room in a mountaintop restaurant. What began as a business meeting soon turns into something else, and the pair falls, tentatively, in love in "Mountain Duet," a lovely ballad for two that captures the spirit of Amor on a shimmering moonlit Alpine night.

Florence comes back, and in "Florence Quits" abandons the American in favor of her new Russian lover. Her bitter confrontation with her erstwhile partner is one of the show's great throwaway melodies, a rockin', stompin' chorus that will return in a similarly acerbic context in the second act.

Enamored of Florence, the Russian attempts to defect to the West, and in a comic number, "Embassy Lament," a pair of contestants for the Upper Class Twit of the Year competition, otherwise known as British Civil Servants, complains of the increase in paperwork occasioned by defections. "Though we're all for/Basic human rights it makes you wonder/What they built the Berlin Wall for."

The first act ends with the stirring patriotic "Anthem," in which the Russian sings that, while he may be defecting, no land will ever replace his homeland in his heart. The song is, probably intentionally, evocative of Elgar's "Land of Hope and Glory," and speaks to every man's love of hearth, home, and country. Which, of course, left many puzzled about *Chess*'s true political leanings; despite perestroika, how could a show be so sympathetic to the bad guys?

But it is. The second act opens a year later, in Bangkok, where the victorious Russian is to defend his title against a new challenger from the Soviet Union. And there, of course, is the American, covering the match for television and hymning (and deriding) the fleshly joys of the Thai capital in the hit song "One Night in Bangkok." Back in her hotel, Florence muses on her deteriorating relationship with the Russian in the tender "Heaven Help My Heart."

Things immediately get worse when the Russian's wife, Svetlana, flies in from Moscow to stand with her husband in his hour of need. In a nasty "Argument," they split up, at least for the duration of the tournament. What follows, a duet for the two women called "I Know Him So Well," is Rice's finest accomplishment, a heartrending reflection on the inherent impossibility of human happiness whose harsh sentiments are underscored by a musical setting that unfolds from a simple beginning to a shatteringly bleak climax. "Wasn't it good?/Wasn't he fine?/Isn't it madness/He won't be mine?/Didn't I know/How it would go?/If I knew from the start/Why am I falling apart?"

At this point, plotwise, the show bogs down into a complicated psywar exchange having to do with the American's blackmailing of the Russian with negative information about Florence's father's activities during the 1956 Hungarian uprising against the Soviets. It doesn't matter. (Nobody really knows what happens at the end of *The Marriage of Figaro*, either.) Suffice it to say that the American, frustrated by the loss of Florence to his archrival and unable to get her back either by hook or by crook, launches into the most moving aria of the show, the fierce "Pity the Child."

This brilliantly constructed number examines the American's unhappy childhood: a broken home, an absent father, an uncaring mother with a succession of interchangeable lovers, the loss of any kind of human contact that might have made him a rounder, fuller person. The *Times* critic sneered at the sentiments, but "Pity the Child" is an emotionally devastating song that builds in intensity until the American reaches the final, chilling realization: "Pity instead the careless mother/What she missed/What she lost when she let me go/And I wonder does she know/I wouldn't call—a crazy thing to do/Just in case she said who?"

"Pity the Child" is the high point of *Chess,* at once its finest song—the concluding hostile rock guitar solo alone is worth the price of the album—and the summation of Rice's bitter world view. The plot winds down in "Endgame" as the Russian handily defeats his challenger, but realizes that, in winning, he has lost both Florence and Svetlana. Nobody's on nobody's side: as the show concludes, the American is alone, Florence is alone, Svetlana is alone, and the Russian is alone. "You and I/We've seen it all/Chasing our hearts' desire/But we go on pretending/Stories like ours/Have happy endings." Yes, and have a nice day!

So maybe now it's clear why *Chess* failed commercially, at least on stage. (The album was a big hit, and one of the songs hit the Top of the Pops.) With a cynicism worthy of Da Ponte, Rice tackled the thorny problems of modern love and relationships and came up with no solutions. Don't trust love, because it is preordained to fail; don't put your faith in other humans, because nobody's on nobody's side. It's not a Barnum-and-Bailey world; it's a dog-eat-dog world, and the sooner we all learn that the better we'll all be. Such at least is Rice's gloomy weltanschauung.

Is that, however, so very different from *Così*? The eighteenth century was no less contemptuous of the folly and impermanence of relationships, and Da Ponte's tale about the pair of young men who switch lady friends on a dare and discover that it is just as easy to fall in love with one girl as the other is nothing if not skeptical. And *Così* is a comedy! We are supposed to laugh as the silly women fall for the patently transparent "Albanian" disguises donned by the lads and then are thrown into consternation at the end when the masquerade is revealed and they are supposed to return to their original partners as if nothing had ever happened.

Is *Chess* really that tragic? If you accept Rice's premise, then what follows is unavoidable, the working out of a not-so-divine plan for human unhappiness that, when you stop to think about it, is comic in the humanistic sense. At the end of *Chess* each character has played his or her best gambit and either won or lost. The Russian has his ambition; the American has his misery; Florence has her uncertainty. And aren't they each, in their own way, happy in their unique unhappiness?

This is where music enters the picture. Looked at coldly, on the printed page, Rice's lyrics seem insupportably bleak: run, don't walk, from this musical. But the Andersson-Ulvaeus score ameliorates them, bathes them in the balm of lyricism, makes them seem, if not universal, at least plausible—and not all that unhappy. The final song, "You and I," which leaves all the principals as lonely as clouds, is disarmingly warm; outfitted with different words, the music might just as easily express the Triumph of True Love—not!

The fact is that "You and I" is the sadder-but-wiser lyricism of the last act of *Figaro,* or the celestial trio of Richard Strauss's *Der Rosenkavalier,* not the comic concluding romp of *The Barber of Seville.* Indeed, the last notes are sounded on the horns, which opened the show in such bucolic splendor a couple of hours earlier. This is music of resignation and of acceptance; it is music for grown-ups, not children, in which "stories like ours have happy endings" only in fairy tales, and nobody lives happily ever after.

Is *Chess,* then, an opera? It certainly deals with classically operatic subjects, and does so in a classically operatic way. It forwards its plot through entirely musical means, offers each character one or more set pieces through which to express his or her inner nature. For all its dramaturgical flaws, which proved insuperable on stage, it communicates its fundamental message clearly. Its orchestral interludes are well crafted and affecting, its ensembles stirring. If it walks like a duck and quacks like a duck, it's probably a . . .

Well, who cares what we call it? The point of this chapter is that it doesn't matter. We must judge any work that makes pretensions to art fairly and evenly, without worrying into which category it may ultimately fall. Is *Chess* an opera? I believe it is, but it's not my job or yours to determine that. Instead, it's up to us to listen to it with an open mind, to evaluate it on its own terms—does it succeed in what it set out to do?—and to send it packing off to posterity with our provisional value judgments slapped across its hindquarters, there for posterity to make up its own mind.

The operatic repertoire is littered with the corpses of once-esteemed works and composers (Giacomo Meyerbeer, take a bow!) that have fallen out of favor. *Robert le diable* was once the bee's knees of opera, so famous that Liszt's pianistic paraphrase was demanded as an encore at practically all of his concerts. Today, it nestles comfortably in history's circular file, along with most of Meyerbeer's other grand operas, including *Le prophète, L'étoile du nord,* and *Le pardon de Ploërmel.* Does that diminish Meyerbeer's unquestioned dominance of the French operatic scene in the mid-nineteenth century? No? But neither does it make him a force to be reckoned with today, as Wagner (who, for jealously anti-Semitic reasons, came to despise Meyerbeer) continues to be.

I can't predict the fate of *Chess* or any of the other Broadway scores with delusions of grandeur—or of any straightforward serious opera. *Porgy and Bess* seems to have shouldered its way into the repertoire, although I have never been a fan of that particular score, whose liberal good intentions sound today painfully contrived and obvious. Leonard Bernstein's *Candide* is another Broadway show that has made the transition to the opera house without much fuss, and yet, for all its huffing-and-puffing high spirits, it's not half the effortless masterpiece that *West Side Story* is. Indeed, the latter show's perfect book and apposite Sondheim lyrics complement the genius of Bernstein's music in a way that ought to have been a model for every so-called serious composer of the time—but wasn't, thanks to the "high-class–low-class" separation. In fact, it was just this separation that turned Bernstein from the correct career path of *West Side Story* to his "serious" works such as the *Mass.* Poor Lenny, so wise and wonderful about so many things musical, fell for the oldest trick in the book, and spent much of his compositional life trying to be something he was not.

It's not that he didn't have a model right before him in Jerome Kern's magnificent *Show Boat.* This seminal 1927 show is not only the first great modern Broadway musical, it may well also rank as one of the first great American operas. (Its contemporaries in Europe included two masterpieces, Alban Berg's *Wozzeck* and Puccini's valedictory *Turandot.*) In scope and ambition, there is nothing quite like it; not even *Porgy and Bess,* which it superficially resembles, approaches it. Not only did Kern create ravishing standards like "Bill" and "Can't Help Lovin' Dat Man" for the show; in "Ol' Man River" he wrote what is very likely the greatest song yet composed by an American, a Schubert-like strophic composition at once so simple and so perfect that it defies improvement.

What if Bernstein had stood by *West Side Story*? Might not the course of American opera have taken a vastly different turn? If composers younger than Bernstein had seen him take a courageous stand against the forces of false dichotomy and write the music his heart dictated, and not his head? We might have been spared twenty-five years of arid, academic claptrap from the likes of Leon Kirchner and the retro-neo-pseudo-Puccinisms of Gian Carlo Menotti. Alas, it was not to be, and the rock-influenced (and Indian-influenced, and Nadia Boulanger–influenced, etc.) revolution of Philip Glass had to wait until the 1970s.

So the next time you find the tune of "Maria" springing to your lips—not to mention "Pinball Wizard" or "Don't Cry for Me, Argentina" or "Make Believe"—remember that what you are singing is opera. Don't let that bother you. It doesn't really matter what we call it, as long as we recognize it for what it is. As Shakespeare said, a rose by any other name would smell as sweet.

Chapter 7

On Singers and Singing, or Why Are They All So Crazy?

A vile beastly rottenheaded foolbegotten brazenthroated pernicious piggish screaming, tearing, roaring, perplexing, splitmecrackle crashmecriggle insane ass of a woman is practicing howling below-stairs with a brute of a singing master so horribly that my head is nearly off.

—Edward Lear

The good singer should be nothing but an able interpreter of the ideas of the master, the composer.

—Gioacchino Rossini

Let but thy voice engender with the string,
And angels will be borne, while thou dost sing.

—Robert Herrick, "Upon Her Voice"

How hard is it to be an opera singer? Don't you just open your mouth and sing? It may look that easy, but it's not.

Why not? Can't we all sing, if only in the privacy of our own shower stalls? Don't we all fantasize, at least once in a while, about standing up on a stage and belting out a tune, if not like Pavarotti or Sutherland, then at least like Elvis or Madonna? Admit it: every time Bob Dylan opens his mouth, don't you think you can sing better than he does? (You probably can.)

Certainly, it is true that some folks are blessed from birth with beautiful voices, the way others have been gifted with extraordinary athletic talent. A voice is not something that you suddenly find you have in your twenties; almost without exception every major singer has discovered this remarkable instrument lurking within at a relatively early age. Now it is true that voices change and mature as the body does. So generally, you must wait until puberty has finished wreaking its hormonal havoc before you can find out exactly what kind of a voice you possess. Boy sopranos, for example, do not necessarily grow up to be fine tenors. (During the baroque period, the best boy sopranos often grew up to be, with the timely application of the surgeon's knife, men sopranos).

Indeed, the voice is so intimately tied up with the body's age and physical condition (and why not?) that the training of singers involves a kind of detailed, practical medical knowledge that is not necessary in the education of any other musical performer. Singers, in fact, almost never outgrow their need for some kind of outside consultation, whether educational or medical. Indeed, even in mid-career a professional singer will sometimes return to the studio of his or her vocal master for some brushup lessons or to correct any bad habits that may have crept in. Invariably, singers are on a first-name basis with the same handful of doctors, most of them in New York City, who specialize in the care and feeding of the vocal chords. (One legendary operatic M. D. was Leo P. Reckford, a Viennese immigrant born Leo Recknitzer, who came to New York City in 1939 and quickly became one of the leading practitioners of "phoniatrics.") Singers are widely regarded to be irrational hypochondriacs when it comes to their instruments—and they have to be, purely in self-defense.

A singer almost never refers to "my voice." It is always "the voice," a mysterious, ineffable creature lurking somewhere between the diaphragm and the adenoids upon which the artist wholly depends for his or her livelihood. It is a semisymbiotic relationship, in which the voice is a parasite and the singer merely the host creature; the voice demands, and the singer gives. It may seem an affectation for Pavarotti to wander around at the height of summer with a scarf wrapped around his zillion-lira throat, but for him it's no joke. The slightest hint of a cold sends a singer into a state of sheer terror, especially in these days of incessant jet travel. Airplanes and colds have a relationship akin to gasoline and lighted matches, and singers positively dread the prospect of flying if they're even a tiny bit sick. Because when they get off the plane at the other end, what started as a sniffle can become a raging head cold, provoking the familiar preperformance announcement, "Ladies and gentlemen, although Miss Pazzo is indisposed, she has graciously consented to . . . " (Cheers from the audience, excellent notices from the critics the next day, etc.)

Imagine what it would be like for you to go to work each morning and not know whether the tools you need to do your job are actually going to be there. Imagine walking into your office on the day of a major presentation and finding everything gone—no computer, no desk, no telephone, no secretarial services, nothing. Or, maybe even worse, they're all there, but in horribly decrepit condition and wholly unable to do the job, although they can approximate it. And only you realize it. How would feel then? How would your boss feel?

You'd feel the same way a singer does when she's sick, that's how. Frustrated. Angry. Embarrassed. Humiliated. Maybe even fired. Trying to go on stage to sing opera in anything less than peak vocal condition is to invite possibly career-ending disaster. No wonder they're all insane.

What goes into a great voice? What are the considerations that govern vocal production? Marilyn Horne, a great mezzo, once said that, to her, breathing was 90 percent of vocal technique. Now doesn't that sound simple? What could be more natural to any of us than breathing? And yet, it's not *that* you breathe, it's *how* you breathe that can determine how good a singer you will be.

Horne, who started singing at the age of five, was lucky in that she had a fine teacher who taught her how to stand and how to breathe. If you've ever heard Horne—better yet, if you've ever seen her on stage—you'll already have a vivid image of her technique, because "Jackie," as her friends call her, probably has the best posture of any singer before the public. Horne doesn't just stand; she *plants* herself as if she were rooted to the stage, and (in her words) "thinks out"—that is, thinks about projecting her voice out over the footlights and into the vast recesses of the opera-house auditorium. She succeeds splendidly: whatever one may think of her work as an artist, nobody has ever complained that Marilyn Horne's voice was too small for its venue.

The great baritone Cornell MacNeil, on the other hand, liked to say that you didn't need a teacher to sing. He needed a teacher for all the other aspects of opera, but not for singing, which came naturally to him. "The problem with singing," he told fellow opera star Jerome Hines in Hines's fascinating book, *Great Singers on Great Singing* (1982), "is that people complicate it enormously. It was natural enough to me until I was well into my career. I had to learn things like languages and style. That's what I concentrated on because I didn't really have any vocal problems." He's not alone—such great voices as Adelina Patti, Amelita Galli-Curci, Luisa Tetrazzini, and, closer to our own time, the tenor Mario del Monaco, all were either largely or entirely self-taught.

Others with whom Hines spoke—and his book is a Who's Who of the postwar operatic scene—speak of the relationship of physique to the kind of voice you have (Horne is as powerfully built as her voice), the importance of intelligence in vocal production, the right frame of mind, even the weather. The point being, I suppose, that not even the great singers really understand, or can articulate, what it takes to open your mouth and have a beautiful sound emerge.

In this respect, then, singers are very much like athletes, and it is a comparison they often either welcome or draw themselves. Like athletes, opera singers live with the certainty that their careers are finite; that someday their skills will abandon them; and that no matter how much intelligence, stamina, etc., they may still possess, all those other qualities are as nothing once the voice itself has vanished.

Like athletes, too, singers do not know the day and the hour of their professional demise—and, indeed, it may occur so gradually that the last person to notice is the artist himself. How many times have we heard the refrain from a washed-up ball player that "I'm in the best shape of my life." And that, in fact, may be the case; most sports figures, blessed with the careless ignorance of youth, never to stop to ask themselves whence came their talent until it has left them. Since it was always there, they wrongfully assume it will always be there; the thought that it might forsake them is unimaginable. And so our last memories of them are often of the once-great quarterback, sitting on his duff, while men ten or twenty years his junior celebrate his downfall, like a warrior tribe that has just vanquished an enemy chief.

The same goes with singers. Though canary fanciers may cheer the innumerable "farewell" performances of their favorite stars—Sutherland, to take the most recent example, seemed to stagger on for years, ever-more-cleverly redefining the meaning of the word—the rest of us generally find the charms of out-of-tune, wobbly singing highly overrated. But who (besides us congenitally nasty critics) has the courage to inform a singer when he or she is washed up? Damn few opera-house managers or conductors, that's who.

James Levine, the artistic director of the Met, presents an interesting defense. In his younger years, Levine routinely hired singers who were, to put it charitably, past their prime. He did this partly to realize one of his childhood ambitions, to make music with these men and women he had grown up admiring. But a more important reason, in his view, was to present a vanishing kind of vocal artistry to the public before it disappeared altogether. It was worth it, Levine felt, to hear Renata Scotto at something less than her best in order to show younger audiences the way opera used to be sung. It's an argument you can certainly dispute, but that's the way he felt.

Eventually, though, Father Time comes calling for everybody. While operatic careers tend to last longer than sports careers, the renewal of the art form constantly demands a fresh influx of talent. So it is all to the good that careers come to an end, that singers learn to bow out gracefully. Because the ego is closely wrapped up in any discussion of an opera singer's psyche, however, it is almost impossible to convince a singer that work, age, and the change of life that hits after the age of fifty have taken their toll. Unlike today's surly, spoiled, and far-too-well-remunerated sports figures, opera singers still thrive on the coin of public adulation, and you would have better luck cutting back their fees than cutting off the applause in which they love to bask. There is nothing wrong with this; it takes extraordinary courage (as well as extraordinary talent) to stand up on stage for more than three hours in what must be the single most difficult performing art. But it does complicate any rational or dispassionate assessment of the state of an individual voice.

Now there's a word hardly ever used in operatic discussion—dispassion. Opera fans are madly passionate about everything operatic, but no single subject gets their juices flowing the way a knock-down, drag-out comparison of great voices, past and present, does. In any group, there will be those who ardently praise today's crop of divas and star tenors; they are opposed by an even larger cohort that claims that contemporary stars are not a patch on the great voices of yore—Tetrazzini, Chaliapin, Caruso, Melba, the De Reszke brothers: the good old days, when men were men and the ladies had chicken dishes and fruit desserts named after them. The fact that there are few or no recordings extant by some of the voices cited is of no moment whatsoever. Indeed, a golden-age singer's reputation is often in inverse proportion to evidence actually in existence.

Were the singers of (pick any historical period) better than today's? So much nonsense has been occasioned by this question, and so much snobbism, that it's time to set the record straight. And the answer is yes and no.

Let me explain. The notion of a golden age is a fundamental fiction, dating back to the Garden of Eden. Things were worthier in the old days, goes this line of thinking: people were smarter, the air, food, and water were purer, streets were safer, everything was cheaper, and, damn it, the opera singers were just plain better too. Never mind that, upon inspection, this premise usually dries up and blows away. (Can you imagine what the sanitation conditions were like in the Garden of Eden, not to mention the moral climate, with all those lions lying down with lambs and Adam and Eve running around buck naked?) The notion of a golden age has a powerful appeal because we can console ourselves with the thought that someday even our own horrible times will be looked back upon fondly—if only by us, in our dotage.

You may begin to suspect, then, that I am not a card-carrying member of the L'Age d'Or Society, especially when it comes to opera. The reason is that I am highly suspicious of recordings, which provide a simulacrum of performance but are (when you stop to think about it) almost entirely fraudulent as a reflection of artistic achievement.

By fraud, I don't mean that the name on the label does not correspond to the sound of the voice on the recording. I accept the fact that if it says it's Caruso, then it's Caruso—although perhaps he's a bad example since, as modern opera's first great superstar, he recorded so much. Instead, I mean it in two senses:

First, the picture of this particular operatic golden age (roughly the turn of the century) that emerges from recordings is highly arbitrary. Recording was in its infancy then, and not every great voice took to it. Some singers made plenty of Edison cylinders and acoustic recordings; others made few or none at all. Further, the limitations of the medium itself circumscribed the scope of the material. It simply was not feasible to record all of Wotan's Farewell from Wagner's *Die Walküre* on an Edison cylinder, so a lot of encores and bon-bons got recorded instead. The early recordings were also incapable of capturing the auditory range of an orchestra, and so instruments that sounded better were often substituted, with a resulting musical distortion. Finally, it was rare for more than two singers to record together, and so we have little idea of how any of the golden age voices functioned operatically, as opposed to merely vocally.

We can, of course, extrapolate—and some do. Of course certain qualities, or lack of them, are audible on the old recordings. Alma Gluck, the Romanian-born American soprano who made her Met debut in 1909, emerges as an adequate but unremarkable soprano, while Emma Calvé is electrifying. The voice of the great Caruso (to my ears) seems oddly ordinary, although his musicianship is impeccable, whereas his great contemporary, John McCormack, sings with a technique and interpretative insight unmatched among lyric tenors of today. Hear Giovanni Martinelli, perhaps the most important immediate successor to Caruso, sing Lensky's aria from *Onegin* (in Italian) without the slightest sense of Russian style; listen to the ravishing Maria Jeritza in an aria from Erich Wolfgang Korngold's *Die tote Stadt,* and weep. And yet, from this selective evidence, some critics and vocal historians have constructed huge castles in the air as they wax rhapsodic about various obscure (to the layman) figures from half a century ago and more. They may be right; they may be wrong; they may be crazy. The thing is, we can't really ever know for sure. Which is, I suppose, part of the fun.

Let me interject something at this point, which will be of special interest to *Phantom of the Opera* fans. If you have read the novel, you know that one of the principal characters is the magnificent Paris Opéra itself, designed by Charles Garnier and one of the glories of musical architecture anywhere in the world. Gaston Leroux, the author, took great care in getting his setting exactly right, and if you have ever actually been inside the Opéra, you will know that Leroux's description is right on the money.

"Even the lake?" you ask. Yes, even the famous subterranean lake. But of more interest to our discussion here, Leroux also tantalizingly mentions a cache of gramophone records buried on one of the Opéra's underground levels. In the book, it is just outside this room that Erik the Phantom's skeleton is found at the end. I always assumed the trove to be fictional, but during a stem-to-stern tour of the Paris Opéra I made in 1987, I discovered to my surprise—and the surprise of my tour guide—that it was not. On the dusty old door of a locked and sealed room is a plaque that reads: "Gift of M. Alfred Clark, 28 June 1907. The room in which are contained the gramophone records." It is a time capsule, not to be opened until the year 2007. And what does it contain? It's impossible to know for sure, but Alfred Clark was the director of the Berliner Record Company in Paris, so we have to assume that the chamber holds a sampling of his company's wares. When it is finally opened, it may well prove to be the single most important collection of turn-of-the-century French vocalism ever unearthed; so far, hélas!, the Opéra administration has rejected all petitions to open it up.

Closer to home, every artist of any reputation or accomplishment is represented on LP and CD. Selectivity is not the problem here: studio wizardry is. Which brings us to my second objection to recorded performances. Ever since Glenn Gould demonstrated the alternative reality of the recording studio, musicians have employed recordings in an extramusical way to create in sound what is impossible to duplicate on the stage. Thus Herbert von Karajan, another who understood that recordings were not live performances and vice versa, could get Mirella Freni, who is fundamentally a lyric soprano, to essay Aida on record. I once asked Freni why Karajan had picked her for one of Verdi's most challenging roles. "The maestro said to me, 'Mirella, I no like Aida screaming,'" she replied. In other words, she could sing at what for her was a normal volume, and with her normal method of tone production, and not have to worry about filling the Metropolitan Opera House or the Grosses Festspielhaus in Salzburg, two huge auditoriums. The recording engineer would do it for her. So is Freni a great Aida? Can she even sing Aida? Once again, the answer must be yes and no.

These are two of the reasons I distrust recordings, and why I tend to discount much if not most of the enthusiasm for the golden age. But the most important reason by far is that, in longing for a never-never land that perhaps never was, we ignore the very real operatic strengths of our own time. In fact, I think a strong case can be made that opera has never been better.

Modern opera singers get up every morning and start to vocalize with one tremendous disadvantage. Unless they specialize in new music (and almost nobody does), with each passing year they get further away in time from the wellsprings of their repertoire. When Tetrazzini et alia were active, they were singing music by composers who, if not actually still alive, were only freshly interred. Everybody always makes a big fuss about Arturo Toscanini, who was indisputably a great conductor. But when Toscanini conducted the world premiere of (among other things) Puccini's *Turandot,* he was leading music by a man who had been known to him personally. He didn't have to imagine a connection to Puccini's time, place, and ethos; he shared it. Without having to find it in the score, he knew exactly what Puccini meant by this musical gesture or that. So much of musical performance in the past relied on the composer's confidence that he didn't have to spell everything out for his performers that it is hard for us, as we debate whether the tenor should or should not try to interpolate a high C at the end of the first act of *La bohème,* to imagine that the answer used to go without saying.

But why shouldn't this be true? In our time, every garage band from Savannah to Seattle shares a rock and roll lingua franca not only with its contemporaries but with the great bands of the fifties and sixties. They no more need to have rhythmic practices notated than they need to think to breathe. And so it was with the golden-age performers. They were singing and playing music of their time; today's opera stars are not.

And yet, I would be very surprised if, in any hypothetical battle of the bands between the best of today's singers and the golden agers, the modern singers did not hold their own. Certainly, to take just two examples from the tenor range, Pavarotti and Domingo are the equal of any of their predecessors in just about any category you care to name. Even McCormack and Beniamino Gigli, two famously gorgeous tenor voices, were not Pavarotti's equal in sheer beauty of sound; even Caruso probably could not match Domingo in the power of his voice or in the astonishing range and breadth of his repertoire. Faced with their built-in handicap, today's singers not only have to sing better than their forebears, they have to sing smarter. And, by and large, they do.

Like modern baseball players, modern opera singers are also faced with conditions that an earlier generation could not imagine. They fly vast distances, jump off airplanes, and perform the most demanding roles, hardly batting an eye. They deal with a constantly shifting group of colleagues and somehow forge a sense of ensemble. They confront widely varying acoustical conditions as they travel around the world's great opera houses. It is the musical equivalent of making Babe Ruth suddenly play a day game after a night game on an eight-game West Coast swing; face a fresh relief pitcher throwing ninety-five miles an hour in the ninth inning; and deal with the postgame interview on ESPN, in which he gets to watch himself strike out with the bases loaded and then tell the interviewer how he feels. Given these circumstances, and the toll they take on the mind and body, it must be admitted the modern singers stack up very well indeed.

Another area in which modern opera performance seems to me superior is in the overall musical preparation. Here, the cultural disadvantage of being removed in time from the source becomes a musical advantage. Singers, conductors, and orchestral musicians know the scores they play practically by heart, and they perform them with a degree of technical accuracy that was simply beyond the capabilities of an earlier generation.

Then there are modern opera's production values. The past several decades have witnessed the rise of the director as an integral part of opera, and contemporary singers are called upon to be singing actors as well as great voices. Tell that to McCormack, who was positively wooden on stage, or any of his colleagues, who were apostles of the stand-and-deliver school of dramaturgy. Few earlier singers worried or cared much about dramatic nuance or psychological insight. But today's discerning audiences have come to expect precisely that from new opera productions, so not only do performers have to worry about musical values, they now must occupy themselves with dramatic considerations as well. Naturally, these are still secondary. Nobody really expects Pavarotti to turn into a singing Olivier at this stage of his career, and given a choice between a great singer who acts a little and a great actor who sings a little, opera audiences still rightfully insist on the former. Still, you get an idea of how complex this business of opera has become and can spare a little sympathy for the poor singers.

At root, however, singing today is not much different from singing a hundred or two hundred years ago. The opera houses, especially in America, are certainly bigger than any Mozart ever encountered or envisioned, but the vocal mechanism remains innately human, and thus pretty much the same as the day Og the Caveman sang the first "Air on the Death of a Mastodon."

Because of where their instrument is located, singers must understand its mechanism in a way that pianists do not need to. A pianist sits down at the keyboard and plays; if he doesn't like the way it feels or sounds, he calls the tuner or the technician to fix it. He doesn't need to know a thing about pins and sounding boards and straps and flanges and all the other paraphernalia of the piano. He should know something, of course, but it's not absolutely vital—unlike the situation for, say, oboists, who have to make their reeds and thus are more intimately connected with the quality of tone production they get from their instruments.

The singer, though, must face up to such physiological aspects as:

- The breathing mechanism, including respiration; the thorax; the diaphragm; the lungs; the abdominal muscles, including the internal and external obliques and the transversus and rectus abdominis; the latissimus dorsi; blood circulation; and even such arcana as unphonated alveolar pressure.

- The laryngeal mechanism, which controls pitch, including the vocal cords and their attendant tissues, such as the thyroid and cricoid cartilages; the cricoid-thyroid, arytenoid, and thyro-arytenoid muscles.

- The resonators, including: the ethmoidal, frontal, and maxillary sinuses; the naso, oral, and laryngeal pharynxes; the nasal cavity and the mouth and tongue.

Once a singer grasps the foundations of his or her voice, he or she must learn how to control it. Understanding how the body works, and why, is just the prelude to actually mastering the complex processes that occur when a singer opens his mouth. Breath control, as Jackie Horne points out, is a large part of the singer's technique, and the control of intrathoracic pressure is the basic bottom line of singing. From this evolves the mastery of pitch and dynamics that all great singers possess.

And yet, there is something that not even the greatest of singers can do anything about, and that is the inherent quality of the voice itself. What is the difference between Gigli and the hundreds of other tenors active in the twenties and thirties? Setting aside all questions of taste and technique, Gigli just sounded better, that's all. In the end, it may be something as simple and unalterable as the tunable and untunable cavities within one's skull. It is inside these cavities—the holes in your head, as it were—that vocal resonance occurs, helping to impart each voice's distinctive and unique sound. And there's not a damn thing anyone can do about them, short of trepanning.

This whole subject of singing is inordinately tricky, but that's one of its beauties. Because there are almost an infinite number of variables that go into it, there will never be total agreement as to what constitutes great singing or a great operatic performance. Accordingly, rival performance factions have long existed in opera, paralleling the endless words-or-music debate among composers.

Was Maria Callas a greater soprano than Renata Tebaldi? In the 1950s, you could practically get into a fistfight on the subject. Callas, her partisans would assert, was the foremost singing actress of the day, a performer of such dynamism and magnetism that you could forgive her various technical deficiencies and luxuriate instead in the force of her characterizations in such roles as Norma. (Translation: so what if she can't sing?) Oh yeah? retorted the Tebaldi fans. Our girl may be a statue, but she's a beautiful statue with a ravishing voice, and what do you go to the opera for, anyway? (Translation: so what if she's a cigar-store Indian?)

Who was right? Once again, the answer is a hedge: both of them, as it turns out. Callas was very much a you-had-to-be-there singer, apparently. I wasn't, and so my exposure to her artistry has come through recordings. And on records, she isn't much. Her many vocal problems, which were partly exacerbated by her offstage diva antics, including her tempestuous romance with Aristotle Onassis, simply overwhelm whatever musico-dramatic points she is trying to make. Without the corporeal presence of the woman, the voice seems disembodied and adrift; if Callas's recordings were an audition tape, she wouldn't get the part.

By contrast, Tebaldi holds up marvelously on records; you can listen to her sing for hours and never get tired of the sound. But I am too young to have seen her on the stage, and from all accounts she wasn't much of an actress. To be fair to her, she came up in opera at a time when you didn't have to be; to be fair to Callas, she reinvented the whole notion of what it meant to be an opera singer. On balance, then, Callas is the more important figure, not only for the way she changed our idea of operatic singing but for her effect on the repertoire as well. Without her Norma, the whole bel canto revival might never have happened.

The same goes today for Pavarotti and Domingo. It is their cruel fate to be locked in eternal contemporaneous lockstep with each other (Domingo is a little younger). But isn't it foolish to try to choose between them? And do we have to? No one can compare in sheer vocal beauty to Pavarotti; no one can compare in overall vocal splendor and musical intelligence to Domingo. Although they are usually lumped together, they actually have little in common beyond a partly shared repertoire. (At this stage of their careers, Domingo's repertoire is probably ten times the size of Pavarotti's.) Opera benefits from both their presences.

And don't think they don't know it. One time I was sitting with Pavarotti in his New York City apartment, talking about his then-forthcoming appearance as Otello, a role he was singing for the first time. I asked him how he was going about learning the score; the music was open on the piano, and I half-seriously inquired whether he would like to run through an aria or two with me as his accompanist. "No," Pavarotti said, "I would be too embarrassed." Come on, Luciano, I said, we're just a coupla white guys sitting around talking Verdi here, no one's gonna know. "No," he said, "I'm not ready yet." Okay, says I, tell me how you're learning the part. For an answer he reached down and brought up—yes, the Domingo recording of *Otello* with Levine. And why not? Nobody sings it better.

Which only goes to show that much of the so-called rivalry between great singers exists largely in the minds of their fans. Callas and Tebaldi were surely smart enough to realize that each benefited from the existence of the other; that they were complementary figures, not antitheses. I have never heard either Pavarotti or Domingo utter a single negative comment about the other, even though they both may harbor private jealousies. Just as there are horses for courses, so are there singers for roles—and audiences for singers. Not everyone is blessed with Joan Sutherland's voice; and yet Sutherland was hopeless in any role that required dramatic impact that was not exclusively vocal. No matter what language she sang in, it all came out mush. Did that make her any less of a singer? Not every role requires the firepower of Sutherland, Callas, Tebaldi, Pavarotti, or Domingo; not every role would be suitable.

And this, in the end, explains the eternal dynamic of singing. If there were no Pavarotti, would Domingo's qualities be thrown into quite such high relief? If there were no Domingo, would Pavarotti, no pun intended, loom quite so large?

For a change, the answer is simply no. Enjoy.

The Opera Experience, or Now What Do I Do?

I hate performers who debase great works of art: I long for their annihilation: if my criticisms were flaming thunderbolts, no prudent Life or Fire Insurance Company would entertain a proposal from any singer within my range.

—George Bernard Shaw

All singers have this fault: if asked to sing among their friends they are never so inclined, if unasked they never leave off.

—Horace, *Satires*, 35 B.C.

The actor apes a man—at least in shape
The opera performer apes an ape

—Ambrose Bierce

You've consulted the schedule, bought your ticket, and settled into your seat. All around you, folks in business threads or evening finery are reading their programs or chatting quietly with their neighbors. Suddenly, you notice the lights are going down and the curtain is going up. Yikes! You're in the opera house! Now what do you do?

Relax. Things aren't as desperate as they seem. In this chapter, we'll walk you through the operagoing experience, letting you know what to expect, when, and why.

Let's begin with an ugly reality: the cost. Opera is not cheap and probably never has been. It costs a lot of money to hire singers, chorus, and an orchestra; to design and make sets and costumes; to own or rent an auditorium suitable for music theater; to assemble a management team and staff. Opera has two characteristics that make it especially troublesome in the lean and very mean nineties: high overhead and an almost zero rate of potential productivity increase.

The overhead can be cut, and opera companies have been doing just that by sharing or simplifying productions, paring and combining staff functions and, more drastically, reducing the length of seasons. But very little can be accomplished in the way of productivity, short of slashing the time it takes to perform, say, *Tosca* in half. ("Do we *have* to do Act Two every night?" "But boss, that's where 'Vissi d'arte' is!") Within a few minutes either way, operas take exactly as long to present in the late twentieth-century as they did in the late nineteenth.

So opera is expensive, and getting more so every year.

The top singers and conductors naturally command top fees; opera companies are notoriously secretive about what they pay a star, but for a run at the Met, the top fee is $12,000 a night. (Someone like Pavarotti or Domingo can earn much more, of course, in solo concerts and one-shot stadium and arena appearances. For the second "Three Tenors" concert in Los Angeles in the summer of 1994, each man, plus José Carreras, reportedly was paid a million dollars.) Orchestras, which are inevitably unionized, are very expensive to operate and notoriously loath to offer any concessions to management.

Thus your ticket may bear a price of $50, $100, or even more. Sure, you can get in cheaper, and most companies hold back some seats for the hoi polloi, or even offer standing room; in German and Austrian opera houses the *Stehplatz* is an old and honored tradition, and one sees the standing areas crammed with students, often armed with scores. Any longtime operagoer will tell you that some of his or her fondest memories are of the days in standing-room, where they saw and heard such legends as (fill in the blanks) for the price of a cup of soup. Still, sitting beats standing any day, especially if your are over twenty-five.

The first question I can hear you asking, therefore, is: is it worth it? Why should I shell out megabucks for a seat at the opera when I can . . . when I can . . . can . . . ?

When you can what? A ticket for a Madonna concert is likely to set you back a bundle, if you can even get one; if you have to go to a scalper, forget about it. Pro football tickets cost as much as opera tix, and even baseball is no longer as cheap as it used to be. Broadway long ago saw its first $100-a-seat show, and no one is surprised any longer when the latest British import sets a new record for costliness.

So stop complaining about sticker shock and think about what you're getting in return. You're receiving the services of hundreds of highly skilled professionals—on the stage, under it, and behind it—most of whom have worked all their lives to achieve the level of artistry you're so happy to witness. Musicians study every bit as long and hard as doctors, and they generally are remunerated at only a fraction of the rate, so don't begrudge them their earnings.

Not only are you helping to support them, you're also supporting opera in your community. Having an opera company in one's town used to be thought a Good Thing; an opera house, it was believed, elevated the tone of the neighborhood and helped local corporations recruit top employees from elsewhere. Alas, in the hateful social climate of America today, this argument will get you an argument in return: opera houses are "elitist" symbols of Dead White European Male cultural hegemony, the money could be better spent on the homeless or the sick or the poor or the nonwhite, blah, blah, blah. Meanwhile, corporations are busy firing middle managers, not hiring them; and who cares about tone anyway, when the role models for our youth are ghetto gangsters who flop around in unlaced sneakers, shoot their best friends, and think lyrics comprised largely of the word "motherfucker" are the second coming of Noël Coward?

Apparently, while I wasn't looking during the five years I spent in Europe, an inane, pernicious collection of "feelings"—we don't have thoughts, or values, anymore, only feelings—has taken root. I suppose this is not the place to get into a discussion of the multicultural society, except to note that opera surely is one of the finest examples of multiculturalism the world has ever seen. And don't kid yourself: the money that is not spent on opera (or libraries or theaters or symphony orchestras) will most assuredly *not* find its way to the homeless or the poor. The next time you hear some moron decrying "high culture" remind him that (a) the poor, as no less a person than Jesus once noted, will always be with us and (b) you have just as much right to your pleasures as Snoop Doggy Dogg has to his.

But let's assume you've smashed your piggy bank and come up with the scratch to buy a ducat or two. The next question (at least from your date) is going to be: what am I going to wear?

Again, relax. You can pretty much wear anything you want, although I must admit to being of two minds on the issue of suitable dress for the theater. On the one hand, you should be comfortable in, and not intimidated by, your surroundings; on the other, you should not look like a slob. The older I get, the more I appreciate my fellow operagoers' dressing like ladies and gentlemen; the opera house is the only venue I regularly frequent where I can sport my tuxedo without being taken for a waiter, and I like that. All men look great in a tux, and there is something about a formally attired audience that promotes bonhomie and good manners. Dressing up for the opera also affords women a bulletproof excuse to buy a new outfit ("Do you honestly expect me to go to the *opera* in this old thing? Don't you want me to look good?"). The tuxedoed gent with the bejeweled lady on his arm makes the perfect operatic couple. Why, it's the next best thing to the high school prom.

Not every night, of course. Nowadays, the rule for formal attire is: on opening night; at the first night of a new production (called a prima, in opera-ese); and at a benefit. In New York City, for example, the Metropolitan Opera has periodic benefits for the Opera Guild, and everyone shows up dressed to the nines, if not to kill. At other times, business attire is fine.

It also depends on where you live. Opening night at the Met, the San Francisco Opera, and the Lyric Opera of Chicago is one of the season's social highlights in each city, but the audiences are radically different. New York draws the crème de la crème, and the crowd is peppered with social mavens, politicians, diplomats, celebrities, and the like. In Chicago, with fewer celebs to go around, the tone is resolutely Middle American (and a little dowdy, it must be admitted), while in San Francisco the large, socially eclectic opera-loving public shows up in everything from tails and top hats to the very latest in B&D leatherwear.

Basically, use your judgment. The exigencies of employment often demand that we come to the opera house directly from the office, and it's perfectly okay for professionals of both sexes to arrive in business suits and dresses. Younger people may want to dress however it is younger people dress these days, which is fine. Just one caveat: keep it clean and, if possible, pressed.

So here you are, in your seat. Before the performance starts, it's a good idea to look over the program. These vary from the pathetic little Stagebills New Yorkers receive to the wonderfully detailed and instructive program books typical in San Francisco, which really deserve to be taken home, studied, and kept. Whichever you get, take a few minutes to familiarize yourself with the cast and with the plot précis, if you don't know the plot and the opera is not being presented with surtitles. Nothing is more annoying to those around you than fumbling with your program during a performance, flipping the pages, holding it up to the light, or, worst of all, idly reading the ads because you're so bored. During the show, the program belongs on your lap, in your purse, or under your seat; it should be neither seen nor heard.

Now to surtitles, or supertitles as they are also sometimes called. I love 'em, and cannot think of a single reason why they should not be used. They are the translations of lines of the libretto projected onto a screen just above the stage, and they have revolutionized the appreciation of opera in this country. Americans are famously averse to foreign languages—oddly, since on the streets of our major cities one can hear forty or fifty different tongues and dialects—and they are just as averse to homework. So telling Americans to read the librettos beforehand and try to puzzle out how the sounds of the Italian or German texts correspond with the English meanings is a hopeless cause. (You should, of course, but I accept the fact that you won't.) The result of this lack of preparation has been generations of American opera-goers sitting in stony silence as Da Ponte's jokes flew by, or scratching their heads at the plot twists of *Il trovatore.*

Enter surtitles, which first came into common use in the early 1980s. From the start, they were loved by the public and hated by some snobbish critics, whose objections against surtitles were basically two. The first, abstract, contention was that by having the text telegraphed, the singers' expressivity was somehow being shortchanged; that having jokes projected on the screen before the words left the singers' mouths in effect ruined the punch line. The second, more practical, objection was that surtitles were (a) inaccurate, (b) infelicitous, and (c) poorly synchronized with the action.

Maybe so. But Protest No. 2 has largely been alleviated through experience. And Exception No. 1 is simply ridiculous. Today, when opera is funny, people laugh—did they ever do that before? So what if they laugh a beat before the singer actually utters the side-splitting line? Is opera some kind of test, on which the audience reaction is being graded for timeliness? Better to have a reaction than to sit there mute and surly.

I'll give you a good example of why surtitles work so well. In the second act of Wagner's *Die Walküre,* which is the second installment in the *Ring of the Nibelung* cycle, there is a very long marital spat between Wotan and Fricka, the chief god and goddess. Outside of German-speaking countries, this long stretch of musical dialogue is greeted with total incomprehension. And yet, it is very important: Wotan and his wife are discussing issues of fidelity and honor that will directly bear on the fate of the human characters, Siegmund and Sieglinde. It's imperative that we understand what they are saying, because otherwise it seems that Wotan is simply being browbeaten and henpecked by his shrewish wife, and that Siegmund must die because his dad just can't take this yenta's yammering anymore.

In the mid-eighties, however, I attended a production of the *Ring* in Seattle, and it was a revelation. For the first time in the many, many *Ring*s I've seen, the audience was wholly caught up in the drama. A flick of the eye, a quick read of the dialogue, and back to the stage: there was not a sound in the house except those Wotan and Fricka were making, nor the slightest sense of the usual is-this-damn-thing-ever-going-to-be-over feeling that one detects during some of the *Ring*'s shall we say less-inspired passages.

The way to handle surtitles is to understand what they are. They are not a literal line-by-line translation of the libretto. There is neither the time nor the space for that. Instead, they offer a sense of what the characters are singing, a guidepost against which you can measure the opera's progress. This is why surtitles are no substitute for your having read the libretto or a good analysis before you sit down, but unless your command of the European languages is impeccable, and your ear supernaturally acute, you'll be glad your crib sheet is right there in front of your nose.

A hush has come over the audience, and now the applause starts to build. You have a moment of panic! What are they doing? Whom are they applauding? You can't see anybody! And why? Nobody's done anything yet!

Calm down. It's only the conductor. And if you're sitting in the orchestra seats (or the stalls or the Parkett), you probably won't be able to spot him until he steps up onto his podium and takes his preperformance bow. It's the folks in the cheap seats who have spotted and greeted him first.

Unlike the symphony orchestra, which performs in full view of the audience, the opera orchestra is located under and in front of the stage. The idea is that the musicians should be heard and not seen—an idea taken to the nth degree by Wagner in the house he designed for his own works in Bayreuth. There, he placed the orchestra completely under the stage, and to make sure no one would be able to see it, he built a "hood" that curves up and over the orchestra pit, shielding it, like a giant prompter's box, from the audience's view. There are few moments more thrilling than the beginning of the *Ring* at Bayreuth; there, the doors are shut, heavy curtains are drawn over the exits, and the auditorium is completely enveloped in darkness. Suddenly, a low E-flat rumbles out of the depths, like some primeval tone, the foundation of the entire universe, and indeed the entire Prelude to *Das Rheingold* emanates from this stygian blackness. Then, at the modulation to A-flat, the curtain shoots up and we see the Rhinemaidens frolicking in the river. My God, they're naked. . . .

Bayreuth is the only opera house in the world where the orchestra is invisible, but elsewhere you're simply meant to ignore it. Sometimes this is difficult, especially when the conductor sets himself up on a high podium, and one is constantly distracted by his halo of hair or his flailing arms. But the only people who really need to see the conductor are the performers, so feel free to ignore him too.

And concentrate on the stage. The big curtain has risen, and most likely what you're now looking at is a choral scene. Many operas begin with a big chorus, be they merry peasants or suffering serfs, and initially you're eye will be overwhelmed by the sheer size of the spectacle. Opera is much, much grander than the average Broadway or West End theater piece, even grander than one of the budget-busting British musicals. Zeffirelli's sets for the Met's production of *Tosca,* for example, are not just sets: they are partial re-creations, at actual size, of the Church of Sant' Andrea della Valle, the Farnese Palace, and the Castel Sant' Angelo in Rome. The only way the sets could be grander would be if they were the actual Roman buildings themselves—and believe it or not, this was actually done during a TV production, broadcast live from Rome a few years ago with Domingo as Cavaradossi.

At this point, if the sets are as grand as advertised, the audience will usually start clapping again. I think this is silly, although the production designer is presumably gratified. But the applause inevitably interferes with the music, so try to restrain your approbation until a more appropriate time—when the act or opera is over.

Another event that often provokes needless applause is moving sets. If your opera house is equipped with the latest in modern technological machinery, the scenery can elevate skyward or sink earthward; whichever direction it takes, it always seems to occasion vociferous cheers from the multitudes. At the Met, this tradition began in the 1960s, with a spectacular staging of Strauss's *Die Frau ohne Schatten* (*The Woman without a Shadow*), and it has continued right up to Zeffirelli's *Tosca:* in the last act, we first see Cavaradossi in his dungeon cell, plaintively singing the famous aria "E lucevan le stelle." The two-stage set is then lowered by the stage elevator and presto, we're atop the Castel Sant' Angelo for the final tragedy. It's exciting. But don't cheer the sets, please. They can't hear you, and it just spoils the music for the rest of us.

This may be a good place to tell you about what happens at the end of *Tosca*. Tosca jumps. Off the top of the castle and, presumably, into the Tiber, although if you've ever been to Rome you know it's an Olympic leap; most probably, she just splats on the sidewalk below. Anyway, the story goes that in one production the soprano playing Tosca duly jumped (onto a hidden mattress)—and bounced right back up in the air. I personally have never seen that, but I was at a performance starring those two sylphs, Luciano Pavarotti and Montserrat Caballé, in which Madame Caballé disdained the jump in favor of the noble offstage waddle: she proceeded in stately fashion into the wings like Queen Victoria sailing down the Nile on a barge.

Sshhh! Somebody's singing.

It might be a soprano. Or maybe it's a tenor. In opera, you will encounter several different types and categories of voice, over which people make a great deal of fuss. You'll hear a lot of talk about a "lirico-spinto" this and a "dramatic" that, usually attached to a familiar word like soprano or bass. But what does it mean?

There are six kinds of voice: sopranos, mezzo-sopranos, altos, tenors, baritones, and basses. Mezzos, who sing slightly lower than true sopranos, and altos, who sing even lower, are often confused with each other, but they're not really the same thing. Neither is a baritone and a bass (the bass is lower), although there is a subspecies called a bass-baritone, which is sort of like a light-heavyweight and countertenor, almost a male alto, who sings in an eerie near-falsetto: the next best thing to a castrato. There are also subcategories, which describe a vocal type or range, such as coloratura soprano (a soprano adept at high filigree singing)and spinto roles, which are simply heavier roles for a soprano or tenor. Almost every opera singer you're likely to hear will be one of these types.

And what are they singing now? Very probably, it's an aria. We've defined our terms in a previous chapter, but now's a good time to review them. An aria is a solo song that usually describes an emotional state; there's not much in the way of plot development in an aria, but we do learn plenty about the character's emotional health (usually shaky) and general state of mind (usually bad). If two principals join forth in song, that's called a duet; three is a trio, four a quartet, and so on up to sextets, septets, and even (rarely) octets. Beyond that it's pretty hard to distinguish one voice from another, so large ensembles basically turn into choruses, which are sung by the servingmaids, spear carriers, sailors, and other supernumeraries who make up the opera chorus.

Acts—there may be one, two, three, four, even five—generally conform to well-tested dramatic shapes, ending on a high (or low) point, with a big aria or chorus rounding things off with a bang. An operatic act can be as short as twenty minutes (Puccini) or longer than an hour (Wagner). Some operas have no intervals at all, either by design (*Das Rheingold, Salome, Elektra, Pagliacci, Cavalleria rusticana*) or by performance tradition (*The Flying Dutchman, Wozzeck*). Sometimes, in order to save time, opera companies will run two acts together with only a brief pause between them, such as between Acts II and III of *Bohème*. In the main, however, the composer and librettist's dramatic plan is observed.

But what if you've bought a ticket to *Rigoletto* expecting to see men in tights and the curtain rises on a lower Manhattan waterfront populated with guys who look like their names are Gino and Fat Tony? In that case, you've wandered into Jonathan Miller's Mafia restaging of Verdi's classic and are getting your first look at radical restaging.

I've covered this phenomenon earlier, but perhaps a few more observations are in order. As the supply of new works entering the repertoire gradually receded—maybe a better way to say it is, as the doors of the repertoire slammed shut on new works—the creativity of opera's interpreters had to go somewhere. You can't expect people as trained and motivated as opera folks to just sit around humming the same tune all day, can you? So directors began to do what directors do best—monkey around, looking for a way to put their own stamp on the material.

Thus we got Despina's Diner (in Mozart's *Così fan tutte*) and *Carmen* set among Hispanic youth gangs in Los Angeles and a modern *Boris Godunov* in which the struggle for the Kremlin is conducted in ill-fitting gray Commie business suits instead of brocaded robes. As I've said before, I have no intrinsic objection to radical restaging—in fact, I tend to be in favor it—providing it is done well.

Miller once told me that in order for him to transpose an opera into a new time and place, he had to be able to find an exact analog. It's not enough to *want* to move an opera from, say, sixteenth-century Florence to twentieth-century Skokie, Illinois. There has to be a correspondence between the two societies that would make the action, drama, and emotions plausible in either place. So when Miller updated *Tosca* by more than a century, setting it in Fascist Italy, it worked. A chief of the secret police (Scarpia, the villain) can be just as villainous in either time, and the opera diva Tosca herself looks just as smart in forties dresses as in Napoleonic-era clothing.

So don't worry if what you're seeing doesn't quite conform to what the libretto or the analysis told you to expect. Go with the flow; be your own critic, and ask yourself how well you think the director accomplished his task. Did it work? If so, why? If not, why not? Not only do individuals have differing opinions, but so do whole cities. Jean-Pierre Ponnelle once staged *The Flying Dutchman* as the dream (or, rather, nightmare) of the Helmsman. San Francisco loved it, but when the production came to the Met, New York practically booed it off the stage and it was quickly dropped. San Franciscans are open to adventure; the Met audience, which prefers its opera sets to be storybook scenes, is not.

But maybe I'm putting the cart before the horse. What you really want to talk about is not whether the director has added anything new to the sum total of human knowledge, or merely vandalized a handsome old structure, but *whether the singers were any good.* After all, isn't that what everybody goes to the opera for?

Not me, as I've mentioned before. But who am I to hold back the tide? You want to talk about singers, we'll talk about singers.

What do we listen for in a voice? Everyone has his or her own taste, but speaking for myself I listen for three things. First, the quality of the voice itself. Is it pleasing?

Do I want to listen to this person sing for the next three hours or would I rather hear a cat being tortured? A voice should be full and rounded and smoothly produced from the bottom to the top of the register; it shouldn't have any obvious holes; it shouldn't wobble; it should be in tune.

Next, how is it being used? Does the singer have any idea what to do with his instrument? Can he color it, shade it, or does he sing every note in exactly the same way, without any thought for the meaning of the material? Is the technique solid? Is the breathing correct? Do I have the sense that the singer is in control of the instrument, or is it likely to crack without warning? I want to feel comfortable with my singers, and so should you.

Finally, what does the singer bring to the party in the way of musicianship? Are the languages being put forth with surety and conviction? Are the dramatic nuances of the character being adequately, or innovatively, explored? Does the singer look good on stage and move well? Is he or she believable in character? Do I like watching him or her on the stage?

It's really not much more complicated than this. In the previous chapter, we got an idea of the enormous complexity involved in the act of singing, but these are the questions you should ask yourself as you sit listening to a performer in the opera house; these are the issues on which you and everybody else will be forming a judgment.

So why not recommend singers? My reason is that singers come and go, and any discussion we get into now is bound to be outdated in a couple of seasons. What good would it do for us to examine the career of Elena Suliotis or Roberta Peters? What interest would you find in an analysis of baritone Robert Merrill (other than as the singer of the national anthem on opening day at Yankee Stadium)? This is why I've been avoiding any direct commentary on the singers of our time, trying instead to focus your attention on the larger issues of opera performance and appreciation.

Fine, you say: tell me who's good. Or who was good. Or who's good that I'm likely to find on records. In other words, help!

Now you're really getting personal. But, if you insist, I'll give you some guidance. The performers mentioned below are some of my favorites, and they may well turn out to be some of yours. Some are still active, some retired; all are well represented on recordings, so you're very likely to run across them as you paw through the record bins and CD stacks. Just remember that opinions are subject to change or revocation without notice, and do not necessarily reflect the views of the management of this publishing house:

Sopranos and mezzos: Leontyne Price, Helen Donath, Hildegard Behrens, Mirella Freni, June Anderson. This is a stylistically eclectic group, but one that covers most of the repertoire. Price was a peerless dramatic soprano, whose Aida and Leonora in *La forza del destino* were without equal. The distinctive coloring of her voice (some profess to hear a "black" sound in it) makes her as instantly recognizable as Ella Fitzgerald, and there was hardly a role she touched that she did not triumph in. Price is a sterling example of how to conduct, prolong, and even milk a career, and she remains a beloved figure in American music.

Donath is an American who did what many American singers did twenty years ago—she moved to Germany, where she married, settled, and built a formidable career. Donath has a delicious light soprano voice, ideal for parts like Sophie in Strauss's *Der Rosenkavalier* (try the Solti recording) or Eva in Wagner's *Die Meistersinger* (try the Karajan); it is impossible to imagine that Donath's best roles were ever sung any better by anybody, anytime, anywhere.

Behrens, at this writing, is pretty well shot, but what a roman candle she was! A German soprano effective in both Strauss and Verdi, she took on opera's biggest dramatic roles—how does Brünnhilde singing "Heil dir, Sonne" while strapped upside down to what appeared to be a giant shield in Peter Hall's disastrous Bayreuth *Ring* production grab you?—and convinced us they belonged to her. She was terrific in the Met's *Idomeneo,* where she even managed to upstage Pavarotti, and no one was ever more convincingly nuts as Elektra in Strauss's great opera.

Karajan may not have liked Aida screaming, but Freni managed to make us forget that her voice was far better suited to Mimi than to the Ethiopian princess. Freni and Pavarotti were both fed by the same wet nurse back home in Modena, and there must really have been something in the Italian water in those days; like the great tenor, Freni ingested a full dose of lyricism that made her suffering Puccini heroines so poignant and affecting. Petite and beautiful, Freni was a far cry—a Pavarotti high note—from the popular image of the opera diva, but nobody comported herself with more dignity than she.

June Anderson looks like Joan Sutherland, and she even sings like Joan Sutherland, but for my money she's a far more interesting and accomplished artist. La Stupenda (yes, Sutherland was actually known by that moniker) was a one-trick pony, a pitcher with a blazing fastball but nothing else. Anderson has all of Sutherland's technique but few of her mannerisms. Anderson uses her voice as a musical instrument rather than as a natural wonder; when she sings Lucia di Lammermoor's mad scene, the listener is primarily caught up in the beauty of the vocal writing, in the emotions of the poor mad girl, and not in the voice itself. She's a real musician, in other words, and in her niche of the repertoire, there are not many who can make that claim.

Mezzos are like viola players in that they don't get no respect, but there have been many great ones, and there is one in particular I would like to single out: the late Tatiana Troyanos. What a terrific singer she was, an artist of grace and depth and accomplishment whose rich Greek-American mezzo could send chills up and down your spine. To her great roles, like Octavian in *Der Rosenkavalier* and Cherubino in *The Marriage of Figaro,* she brought a fierce intelligence and a grand passion matched by few in our time. What a contrast she made to the more refined (and sometimes more affected) singing of Flicka von Stade! The opera world had room for both of them and now, alas, there is only one.

Tenors, baritones, and basses: Placido Domingo, Luciano Pavarotti, José Carreras, James Morris, Samuel Ramey. By now, the "Three Tenors" have become such a phenomenon that I hesitate to even mention them—except that they really are the best tenors around, and two of them rank with the greatest tenors of all time. Carreras is a fine, intelligent singer who, like Freni, was asked to sing roles that were really much too heavy for him; additionally, he was stricken by leukemia and heroically battled back from it to take his place alongside Pavarotti and Domingo in 1990, when the three amigos sang their epochal concert in Rome at the climax of the World Cup.

The day of that concert, with a ticket waiting for me in the Eternal City, I was stuck in Hamburg, trying desperately to find a flight from anywhere in Germany to Rome. But the Germans were playing in the soccer finals that night—they eventually won, as if anybody could possibly care—and so *I was unable to get to the damn concert.* Yes, friends, I now hold the distinction of (a) missing the "concert of the century" and (b) turning down a ride to upstate New York with a bunch of friends in 1969, because who wanted to go to something called "Woodstock," anyway?

Of the other two, what more can one say? Pavarotti is a huge man with what may be the most beautiful Italian lyric tenor voice in history; beside him, Caruso sounds like a barroom belter. No one has ever sung Rodolfo in *Bohème* with more beauty and ardor than Lucianissimo; no one has poured more passion into the now-clichéd aria "Nessun dorma." At his best, which he can still reach, Pavarotti is one of the great vocal wonders of the world, a voice imbued with a special timbre that thrills millions of people all over the world.

(Not that he can't use a little help from time to time, which we critics are happy to provide. When Pavarotti sang his first Radames in *Aida* in San Francisco in the early eighties, I took a dim view of this move to a heavier role, and said so in the pages of *Time*. A few days later, my review was front-page news in the Italian papers: "Luciano: pay attention to your roles!" screamed one headline, pointing that *Time* was looking askance at this lapse in judgment. He dropped the role shortly thereafter.)

Domingo's voice may be less immediately striking, but no less distinctive. Where Pavarotti is lyrical, Domingo is dramatic. His voice has a darker, weightier sound, perhaps betraying its origins as a baritone, but it rings at the top like a true tenor's should, and its flexibility and durability has allowed Domingo to perform an astonishing number and variety of roles. The restless Spanish-Mexican tenor has more than one hundred roles in his repertoire, and he is still adding new ones, in every conceivable style and national school. He sings Puccini and Verdi; he sings Massenet and Bizet; he sings Wagner (Siegmund and, soon, Tristan). Domingo not only sings, he also plays the piano very well, conducts expertly, and has even started to work in operatic administration as a hedge against the day when retirement comes. Pavarotti and Domingo are two of the most remarkable voices of this or any other era: remember that, the next time you hear someone moaning about the lost golden age.

Basses and baritones are inherently less sexy than tenors, but Morris and Ramey are two Americans who have made terrific headway on the international stage. Morris has become one of the great Wotans, a singing actor who illuminates his roles not only with an effortlessly produced voice but with a formidable musical intelligence as well. Ramey is not half the actor Morris is, but his range may be wider, and there is no one to touch him in the Italian basso repertoire.

Obviously, these are only a handful of the noteworthy singers of our time, and it does not even begin to touch on the great singers of the past. There are, however, plenty of books on those subjects if you want to learn more about such figures, and while I do recommend reading, even more do I recommend listening to as many of them as you can and forming your opinions.

Because, in the end, that's what being an opera fan is all about. I would prefer that you save your zeal for the works themselves and not the performers, but if you must, you must, and there's nothing wrong with it. Fandom is what keeps opera houses filled the world over.

And, truth to tell, there are few moments in life more thrilling than the collective hush that comes over an audience when a new voice suddenly emerges from its incubational cocoon and you are there to witness it. Suddenly, there is a sense of excitement and even danger in the air: could it be? Is he, or she, the one? Is this the voice we've been waiting for? Is this the real thing? Can this be . . . love?

And then the cheers sound, rolling over the auditorium like ocean waves. The aria stops, the conductor puts down his baton; the singer steps out of character for just a moment to acknowledge the cheers of the multitude, hand on heart, eyes turned heavenward. When a great voice comes along you'll know it, and you can only hope to be there when it does.

And here you are, sitting in the opera house! It's okay, you can clap now. But don't whistle—in Europe that means you hated it, and remember that many of the singers are European. Better to yell "Bravo!" like that guy in the leather pantsuit next to you.

There, that was easy, wasn't it?

Chapter 9

The Future of Opera, or Where Do We Go From Here?

If I had my way, a young man beginning to compose would never think about being a melodist, harmonist, realist, idealist, musician of the future, or whatever other pedantic formulas the Devil may have invented. Melody and harmony should be simply the means in the hand of the artist to make music.

—Giuseppe Verdi

A composer's first responsibility is, and always will be, to write music that will reach and move the hearts of his listeners in his own day.

—Randall Thompson

The fact is, there are no rules, and there never were any rules, and there never will be any rules of musical composition except rules of thumb; and thumbs vary in length, like ears.

—George Bernard Shaw

There was a running gag about Spain's Generalissimo Francisco Franco on the old *Saturday Night Live* show segment "Weekend Update." The joke was that General Franco was still dead. Week in and week out, the Fascist general, who had seemed to take forever to die, was, thank God, still dead as a doornail. Stiff. Cold. Six feet under. Pushing up daisies. History.

Not so long ago, the same might have been said about opera. Through a coincidental conspiracy of opera haters and fans, the art form, like classical music in general, appeared to be, if not deceased, then certainly on its last legs, a terminal, superannuated exemplar of a dying culture, a prime candidate for the slag heap, the next guest to check into the morgue. Opera's enemies saw it as an outdated, Eurocentric, elitist, and expensive art that (somehow) by its very existence was an affront to the People everywhere. The fans, dwelling in the Neverland memories of their fifties' childhoods, declared that all of modern opera—works, singers, conductors, set designers, and directors—was manifestly inferior to the golden age of their youth; without Callas, life was no longer worth living. At once politically incorrect and artistically moribund, opera was on its way to the glue factory.

What a difference a decade makes. At this writing (1994), opera is without a doubt the most vital performing art around. What once seemed almost ludicrously old-fashioned—fully deserving of its merciless parody by the Marx Brothers in *A Night at the Opera*—has now become the people's choice, the art form with the widest attraction, and the most appeal to younger people. Opera is back, with a vengeance.

Why? What happened? After all the talk about the death of high culture in general and classical music in particular, what has occurred to pick opera up off the mat and send it back, fighting, into the ring? There are probably dozens of reasons great and small, but if you ask me they all boil down to one: composers again started writing music audiences wanted to hear.

By this I do not mean that composers were merely giving people what they wanted to hear. This is what we might call the Pollsters' Fallacy, in which the populace is surveyed as to its tastes, or lack of them, and then presented with precisely what it has just said that it wants. For some reason, the circular reasoning behind this logic has never really been examined, but the baleful results are all too apparent. People know what they know, and they want to know more of the same. It's sequelitis run amok, the substitution of rote for thought, the replacement of intellectual adventure with the safe, dull repetition of experience. As long as we continue to have government by popularity poll, we're going to have presidents like George Bush and Bill Clinton, watching the weathervanes of public opinion in order to "lead." Remember back in your high school elections how the teachers used to say, "It's not a popularity contest"? Well, now it is. And it's just as dumb.

Luckily, music didn't fall into that trap. Once the twelve-tone commies had driven away audiences that had formerly encountered new music not only with tolerance but active enjoyment, they were able to look around and proclaim the unworthiness of the very patrons they had just sent packing. See? I knew you'd hate me sooner or later if I just kept beating you. And like their fellow travellers in the political arena, the "modern music" school then issued edicts akin to the Brezhnev doctrine, which stated that henceforth there was to be no backsliding. The twelve-tone method, also known as serialism, was (like communism) the end result of civilization, the best of all possible worlds, and, once achieved, could never be supplanted. Any hint of revanchism, and tanks would roll.

Well, you know what happened. Serialism is just as dead and discredited as communism, and it couldn't happen to a nicer bunch of guys. (For a fuller discussion of the modern-music problem, please see *Who's Afraid of Classical Music?*) Despite the dire warnings of (among others) college composition teachers across the land—academe, not patriotism, is the last refuge of a scoundrel—what succeeded it was not rewrites of Beethoven and Brahms. At first, maybe: when George Rochberg, a serialist apostate and a pioneer in the humanistic counterrevolution, quoted from earlier composers and then actually knocked off Beethoven in his String Quartet No. 3, it seemed like the Marxist-Leninists might be right. Was this what lay beyond the thorny thickets of dodecaphonism? Traditional harmony? Back to the future? Not exactly. What the naysayers missed was that Rochberg's music was only the beginning; to create a meaningful new tonal system, we had to cleanse our ears of the entire Darmstadt school. We had to return to the market economy in new musical ideas we had so thoughtlessly chucked two decades earlier. Maybe white is white after all.

So ha, ha, ha—composers didn't want to return to writing like Dvořák, and audiences didn't want to hear that anyway; one Dvořák is plenty. What both composers and audiences were longing for was music rooted in their own experiences, but with a twist. Something familiar, yet unfamiliar. They didn't want their noses rubbed in intellectual fascism, but neither did they want the same old pabulum.

And along came Philip Glass. With *Einstein on the Beach* he and Robert Wilson burst into opera-house prominence—much to the dismay of not only the twelve-tone hardliners but also the traditionalists who couldn't make hide nor hair out of the strange new creature called minimalism. Was this opera? Was this music?

A few years later, Glass struck again with *Satyagraha* and created what I guarantee you will be one of opera's enduring masterpieces. Far more conventional than *Einstein, Satyagraha* welded both minimalistic and traditional musical elements into one radiant whole. Yes, the opera wasn't "about" anything. (Actually, it was about a lot, although, since it was sung in Sanskrit, it was hard to tell.) Yes, some of the melodies were simple scales, repeated over and over. (If it was so simple, how come nobody thought of it before?) Yes, yes, yes.

Satyagraha, as I read the history of the eighties, is the single most important work in the revival of new operas in the United States, and maybe worldwide. The hardliners and conservatives might both have hated him, but Glass had a powerful ally in time: he had come to artistic maturity not in the thirties, forties, or fifties, but in the sixties, and he knew everything from Nadia Boulanger and Stravinsky to Ravi Shankar and rock and roll. The opening of *Satyagraha* may have seemed unusual to the fogies, but every kid in the audience heard a standard rock chord progression—albeit played by the string section of a symphony orchestra. And it said: don't be afraid, you're going to like this. There's nothing to it, really, just sit back and enjoy it the way you would any of the other music you like to listen to. They did, and the rest is history.

I spent the eighties based in New York but traveling around the country and the world, and I suppose that if I go back over all the pieces I wrote for *Time* in that decade, maybe half of them had something to do with opera. As I explained earlier, the magazine is predisposed to like opera, but I found myself attending opera on its merits, not because it made for good photographs. Not just new operas, of course, but daring and innovative productions of old ones. All of a sudden, opera was attracting the best and the brightest talents in all its various aspects: singers, conductors, composers, designers, directors. Opera was not only hot, it was sexy; it was where the action was. And it still is.

The past few years have even seen new opera crack the

Met. Glass and Wilson had to rent the house themselves when they staged *Einstein* in 1976; in 1992, it was the Met who invited Glass as it premiered his specially commissioned opera *The Voyage.* That same season, it also offered John Corigliano's *The Ghosts of Versailles,* and had a hit with both. In Chicago, the Lyric Opera began an ambitious program of new American works with William Bolcom's *McTeague.* That premiere attracted critics from across the United States, lured not only by Bolcom but by the opera's director—the canny old Player himself, Robert Altman.

There's still plenty of grumbling, of course, about "distortion" and "trendiness" and other assorted ills. And it's true there have been excesses, especially on the part of producers. I found Sellars's Don-Giovanni-in-Spanish-Harlem more amusing than inspired, for example, and there are far more egregious examples of a director's yanking a work from its original time and place and transporting it elsewhere. Beam me up, Scotty! Some things, however, just don't fly.

And yet, the renewed sense of excitement that now attends opera has rubbed off on more conventional opera productions. A 1994 *Otello* at the Met, directed by Elijah Moshinsky, was emblematic. Outwardly, it might have passed for a staging from twenty, forty, or even sixty years ago. The sets were representational, not abstract; the period was clearly the fifteenth century, not the twenty-first; and Otello was definitely black, not Chinese or Aleutian Islander.

That said, the production could not have been more up to date. Moshinsky knew from the start that this opera, more than most, is about psychological states, and he made sure that the characters reflected their inner lives in deed and gesture. He set up Otello's final collapse in the first act by having the battle-weary Moor hold his head in agony, his guard down, his emotions on his sleeve. Even without overtly signaling that his *Otello* was rethought and reinvented for a late-twentieth-century audience, Moshinsky reinterpreted the opera as surely as if he had transposed it to the moon.

And don't think the performers don't respond. For a production in Bonn, Ken Russell, the outrageous British film and opera director, set Richard Strauss's *Salome* in a Victorian brothel with playwright Oscar Wilde as one of the onlookers; the first music the audience heard was not by Strauss, but by Scott Joplin (the "Palm Leaf Rag," as I recall). At one point, the soprano (Emily Rawlins) singing Salome was raped by the tenor singing Herod, and there was a brief flash of nudity. My, my. And how did you feel about that, Miss Rawlins?

She loved it. Not the nudity per se but the sheer vitality and the originality of Russell's ideas, which infused the whole cast with a sense of purpose and—dare one say it?—a sense of amusement. This is not brain surgery, after all: it's opera, and opera is supposed to be (pick one) shocking, enjoyable, moving, vulgar, snobbish, outlandish, unconscionable, unholy, and downright naughty. All of which Russell's *Salome* was.

Because it's okay to have fun at the opera. Groucho did, but he was having fun at opera's—and Margaret Dumont's—expense. When Irving Thalberg, the boy genius of Hollywood, was cleaning up the Marx Brothers' act—he wanted their movies to be tighter and funnier—he insisted the boys retain their madcap ways but that they act out against the stuffiest background George S. Kaufman and Morrie Ryskind (the head writers) could think of: the opera, of course. And so when Otis B. Driftwood tangles with the snooty Mrs. Claypool at a performance of Verdi's *Il trovatore,* hilarity is the result.

Our kind of fun is different. No one ever said—no one ever should have said—that opera requires some kind of

IQ test before you can enjoy it. All you have to have is the price of a ticket (unfortunately, not in reach of everyone) and an open mind. Sit back and relax; this won't hurt a bit.

For opera is wasted on the opera fans. Why should they have all the fun? Let them parse performances until they drop; you know what you like. Let them debate the relative merits of Madam Tessitura's Tosca until the good lady finally hangs 'em up; what do you care? In the end, the only question that really matters is: do I like this? Is this for me?

With experience comes connoisseurship. All those people chattering mysteriously about spinto roles and head voices and the "break" and so forth—soon enough you'll be able to join them, if you wish. (Frankly, I don't recommend it.) After a season or two at your local opera house, prolonged exposure to your favorite recordings, and maybe a bout with the Met's Saturday-afternoon live broadcast now and then, you'll be well on your way to being an expert.

The point being that opera really should be available to everybody, and if opera is to have a future, it has to be. I'm not so idealistic as to think that if only our citizens were exposed to opera and "good music" at an early age they would all be rabid fans by now. While I deplore the nearly nonexistent state of arts education in this ever-more-philistine society of ours, I don't believe that people find their way to the arts through education alone. A love for the arts is very much like love for a person; you know more or less right away whether this relationship has any future.

So what ought to happen for opera to march smartly into the twenty-first century? Here are my recommendations:

- Keep up the good work. In other words, keep those new operas coming. A young guy named John Moran has written an absolutely terrifying opera called *The*

Manson Family, which has nearly nothing in common with, for instance, Tchaikovsky's *The Queen of Spades*—except that both are sensational music dramas in which madness and violence play major roles. Younger composers have found opera (however broadly defined) to be the perfect vehicle for expressing their thoughts on art and society. It is precisely this social conscience that distinguishes them from their chilly twelve-tone forebears (who, tellingly, didn't write many operas). And it is precisely this same social conscience that has given their work such broad appeal. But wasn't it ever thus?

• Bring ticket prices down. It's hard to see how the opera houses can realistically do this, but that doesn't deter me from recommending it. After living in Germany, I am not one to tell you that the European way is necessarily better. Their system of extensive government subsidy (increasingly under fire as all the European nations start facing up to their social problems) has kept a multitude of theaters, orchestras, and opera houses in business, to be sure, although it seems to me their artists have paid a stiff price in creativity. Still, European audiences are awash in young people—who are the future, whatever the old farts may think of them, their low morals, and their even lower tastes—who present a strong contrast to the sea of blue hair one customarily spies at American concerts and operas. And the way these young folks get in is through the availability of reasonably priced tickets; you can take your date to a movie, or you can take her to the opera. It costs about the same. It doesn't in the United States; in America you not only have to borrow dad's car to go to the opera, you have to sell it.

• Cut the baloney. Opera isn't rocket science, or a cure for cancer, or a new religion. It's an art, something that enables us to examine what it is that makes us human, and as such is terribly important. But it's also a cross between entertainment and a sport, and it's okay to be there even if you're not probing the innermost reaches of your soul. Some show up just to see whether the soprano can hit the high F-natural in Mozart's *The Magic Flute.* Don't begrudge them their little pleasures; life is too short.

• Feel free to boo. Whether it's our famous good manners or our equally famous naïveté, we don't do enough of this. We may scream at our subordinates, spank our kids, and kick the dog, but in the opera house we are mere pussycats. It has gone out of fashion to boo a singer who comes to grief on a high note, and I suppose this is just as well. But it's certainly okay at the curtain calls to let fly with a chorus of disapproval if you think the conductor was a butcher or the director ought to be shot. (It's certainly preferable to actually shooting him.) Exercise your right to choose: if you hated it, express yourself. Just be sure you're hating it for the right reason. Correct: "I hated it because I don't think *Werther* is properly seen as a repressed homosexual love story set in twelfth-century Cambodia." Incorrect: "I hated it because it was sad when Rigoletto stabbed Gilda by accident." In other words, know your grounds for complaint, and whether anything can be done about it.

• Wake up, opera companies. Time to realize that the old ways of doing business just won't cut it anymore. The Lyric Opera of Chicago finally figured this out, and has become one of the most exciting companies around; its old counterpart, the nearly irrelevant La Scala, should only wish somebody called it Lyric Opera East. Time to get busy, commissioning, searching out new works or old ones nobody's heard for a long time. Time to hire the best directors you can find and match them up with conductors who don't sit around wishing they had gone wenching with Puccini. Get the best voices you can find, of course, but

> look for other qualities as well: freshness, beauty, stage presence. Remember, you're not competing with records, you're competing with movies, TV, and the theater, so act accordingly. Put on a show.

That ought to do it. Opera hasn't lasted this long by remaining hidebound. Upon close inspection, many of its most cherished "traditions" (like fat singers) are nothing more than occasion-specific events that have somehow stuck around. Maybe tradition really is just the memory of the last bad performance; in any case, it should never circumscribe the creative efforts of those who have dedicated their lives to put opera on the stage.

In the end, isn't this what opera—or any living art—is all about? Musicians are not priests, docilely reciting a canon. Instead, they ought to be revolutionaries, playing and singing and composing because they have something to say about music. Something to say about the human condition, and how to improve it. Something to say about our society's role in the art form's ongoing history. Something to say not only to our generation but, if they're lucky and good, to future generations as well. Something, in short, to say.

Chapter 

Adventures in the Opera Trade, or The Finale Ultimo

What is music? The very existence of music is wonderful, I might even say miraculous. Its domain is between thought and phenomena. Like a twilight mediator, it hovers between spirit and matter, related to both, yet differing from each. It is spirit, but spirit subject to the measurement of time; it is matter, but matter that can dispense with space.

—HEINRICH HEINE

Music is well said to be the speech of angels: in fact, nothing among the utterances allowed to man is felt to be so divine. It brings us near to the infinite.

—THOMAS CARLYLE

Music is a higher revelation than all wisdom and philosophy.

—BEETHOVEN

In 1986 I was lucky enough to visit the late Union of Soviet Socialist Republics, in the company of Vladimir Horowitz. The occasion was Horowitz's return to the land of his birth for a couple of concerts in Moscow and Leningrad, and *Time* decided the trip would make a terrific cover story, as indeed it did. Of course, the day I arrived the United States bombed Libya, which put a damper on Soviet-American interpersonal relationships, and two days before I left, Chernobyl blew up, which is why I glow in the dark.

Exciting stuff, to be sure, highlighted by the KGB break-in at the American ambassador's residence, Spaso House, and the vandalizing of the ambassador's piano, so Horowitz couldn't practice. But to me an equally memorable moment from that trip was my visit with the Russian composer Tikhon Khrennikov, then the first secretary of the All-Soviet Composers' Union, as well as a candidate-member of the Central Committee of the Communist Party, and thus one of the most powerful men in Soviet music. I had asked for an interview with Khrennikov because he was planning to make a trip to the United States for a Soviet-American music festival, and I thought I would get a jump on the competition. The visit was proving to be controversial: there had already been protests over Khrennikov's participation from those who recalled his leading role in the Resolution of 1948, an official Stalinist denunciation of several prominent Soviet composers that proved a public humiliation for Prokofiev and Shostakovich in particular—by coincidence, Khrennikov's rivals. I was granted an interview, subject to one condition: under no circumstances was I to ask him about that episode.

At the appointed hour, I showed up at the Composers' Union building in central Moscow and was ushered into a large rectangular room dominated by a very long table, at which I took a seat. While I waited, I looked around. The room was plainly furnished, but on the walls hung portraits of several of the greatest figures in Russian music, including Sergei Prokofiev, Dmitri Shostakovich, Aram Khachaturian and Nikolai Miaskovsky. Hmmm. . . .

The door to the room opened and in stalked Tikhon the Great, accompanied by a handful of henchmen, one of whom had a dueling scar running the length of his face; the music biz must be pretty tough here, I thought. Khrennikov turned out to be a short, bullet-headed Slav with tiny eyes that did not twinkle even a little bit. He seated himself opposite me and glared.

The interview was conducted in Russian. I asked first whether he spoke English, and he shook his head vigorously; *Sprechen Sie Deutsch?"* I then inquired, to which he replied vigorously, *Nein!* I turned to my translator and fired away.

It's doesn't matter what we talked about, because his answers were far from forthcoming—banal platitudes laden with Soviet baloney that were both worthless and trite. Khrennikov, interestingly, knew next to nothing about new-music trends in the West, although he did seem vaguely aware of minimalism and even expressed some interest in it. I found myself growing irritated.

"Mr. Khrennikov," I said, "I notice that this room is decorated with portraits of some of the greatest Soviet composers."

"Da."

"Prokofiev, Shostakovich."

"Da."

"I also note that each of these men suffered greatly from the Resolution of 1948, had their careers spoiled, and were put in fear of their lives, partially by your actions."

I could see the steam start to come out of his ears.

"What is your question?" asked Scarface, as if he didn't know. I wondered if he was carrying a gun.

"My question," I said, "is this: how do you, Mr. First Secretary, have the gall to sit in this room in front of the men whose work you denounced and whose lives you tried to ruin and talk about how great Soviet music is?"

Silence. My official translator was trying to disappear into the back of his chair.

"Go ahead," I urged him and, grudgingly, he did.

The effect was electric. Khrennikov leaped to his feet and started pounding the table. "How dare you talk to me like that?" he shouted in Russian, for which no translation was necessary.

He glared at me from his full five-foot six-inch height. Would he storm out? Hit me? Call the KGB and have me clapped into Lefortovo prison posthaste? But no, he was waiting for an answer.

"Because," I said as slowly and calmly as I could, "when you come to the United States, that is the first question you are going to hear, and I thought I would prepare you for the persistence of American journalists in advance."

Khrennikov stared at me for a while, and then sat down—and broke into a big smile. *"Da!"* he said, or words to that effect.

Suddenly, I was his favorite guy. I would of course come to lunch the next day at the Composers' Union (and an excellent lunch it was, too). And I would of course be his guest at the performance that same evening of his famous opera . . . well, I forget which one it was. It might have been *One Hundred Devils and One Girl,* or maybe *White Night.* Whatever it was, it was pretty boring, and my memory of it has largely been reduced to a bunch of peasants in folk costume hopping about.

The point is, you never know when your next operatic

experience is going to come around the bend, and you've got to be ready for it. On that same trip, I visited Leningrad and during one of the Horowitzian off-nights, decided I would visit the famous Kirov Theater that evening. I consulted the Intourist lady in the lobby of my hotel, who informed me there was nothing interesting at the famous Kirov that night. Tomorrow, *La traviata,* but tonight, zip.

"What's this, then?" I asked, pointing to what was obviously the name of something going on at the Kirov.

"Nichevo," she said; nothing.

"No, it's something," I persisted.

"Nothing," she said. "Russian opera."

Now we were getting somewhere. "Which Russian opera?" I inquired.

"I dekabristi," she said, which means *The Decembrists.* "Not interesting."

"Gimme ticket," I said, and that evening I found myself sitting next to my esteemed colleague John Ardoin from Dallas, who was also in town covering the Horowitz magical mystery tour. Ardoin, who is one of the most operatically knowledgeable daily newspaper critics in America, was at the Kirov that night for the same reason I was: to actually see and hear this legendary opera, which to this day has never been produced outside Russia.

John didn't know any more about the opera than I did, but we both sat there entranced. *Dekabristi,* which concerns an 1825 anticzarist revolt in St. Petersburg, was Yuri Shaporin's one and only opera, on which he worked from 1920 to 1953, when it was premiered. The very long gestation period may be explained by the fact that every time the poor son of a gun was ready to bring out his work, along would come another Stalinist blast, like "Muddle Instead of Music" or the Resolution of 1948, and he would hurriedly withdraw it and wait for a more propitious, or at least less dangerous, moment. It was finally premiered in June 1953, three months after Stalin (and Prokofiev) died.

Dekabristi is a big, bold, opulent work that would please any crowd anywhere: imagine a combination of Tchaikovsky, Shostakovich, and Khachaturian and you will have some idea of its musical style. Why some enterprising opera company—New York City Opera? English National Opera?—hasn't gotten its hands on the score by now is beyond me.

Two weeks, two new operas. Once the bug bites, it doesn't stop, and I often go out of my way to catch something new and exotic. Once in Zurich I stumbled across a performance of Heinrich Marschner's spooky *Hans Heiling,* which one certainly doesn't encounter every day. (Marschner is a now-obscure German composer who flourished in the first half of the nineteenth century with such works as *Der Vampyr* and *Der Templer und die Jüdin,* the latter based on *Ivanhoe.*)

Opera has also become a cross-cultural worldwide phenomenon. I have seen Verdi's *Macbeth* staged in a medieval Finnish castle, and Wagner's *Tannhäuser* presented in the giant NHK Hall in Tokyo. In the 1980s I also participated in several U.S.–Japanese music seminars, in both New York and Tokyo, and so it was that I found myself conducting a public interview with the avant-gardist Meredith Monk on the stage of a Tokyo music school prior to one of her performances. On that same trip, I and some colleagues presented a series of lectures on American music theater, a subject the Japanese seemed to find fascinating, and we were treated to several performances of new Japanese stage pieces during our stay, a subject we found fascinating.

Far more than contemporary symphonic music, opera is the best introduction to the world of serious music. Its repertoire encompasses all periods of Western music history, and its creative quotient has not been so high since the late nineteenth century. It attracts some of the finest directors in the world, not to mention the best singers. It takes place in venues that are either opulent and historic, or simply extraordinary—the Finnish castle mentioned above is the home of the annual Savonlinna Opera Festival in northeastern Finland. And of course it is at home in the best cities: London, Paris, Venice, Milan, Munich, Moscow, New York, San Francisco, Chicago, Buenos Aires . . .

If I seem enthusiastic about opera, I am, and I want you to be as well—that's the whole point of this book. What I've tried to show in these pages is that opera may or may not be for everybody, but that's only a matter of individual taste. Once you get past your preconceptions, you'll find there's nothing intrinsic or congenital about loving opera. The operas themselves are so universal in appeal, and speak to such fundamental issues of life, that anyone who chooses to can become an opera fan—in the opera house, if you can afford it and have the opportunity, or at least through recordings. You don't have to be a college professor or a UN translator to love opera. You don't have to know how to read a score—why should you? many famous singers don't—and you don't have to know every word of the libretto.

All you have to do is bring an open mind to the subject. Those of you who read *Who's Afraid of Classical Music?* know that I was raised far from the madding opera crowd and had to work hard to come up to speed. But if I could do it, so can you. It's not that difficult; all it takes is desire.

What I hope you have gleaned from this book, then, is an awareness of the breadth and depth of the operatic repertoire, as well as an understanding of the inner nature of opera. Before we started, you may well have wondered why the tenor takes so long to die, and why everybody always seems to be in love with the wrong person, and why the baritone is always so angry with the soprano. You may have thought that operatic conventions were irredeemably silly, that opera plots were unrealistic and risible, and that the whole idea of listening to someone singing out his or her innermost thoughts was a complete waste of time and money.

I hope by now you're starting to change your mind. Reading this book is only the beginning. Now comes the hard part: going out into the trenches and getting to know the works we've been discussing, and others, and deciding for yourself what opera has to offer you. You really will be glad you did.

A *New Yorker* cartoon comes to mind. (I think it was by Chon Day.) A middle-aged man is lying in bed, the covers tucked neatly and protectively under his chin. He is obviously ill, and his wife is leaning over him solicitously. The caption reads: "I know the doctor says it's only a bad cold, but just in case, I'd like to hear Side Eight of *Der Rosenkavalier* one last time."

Those of you raised on CDs may miss the reference, but Side Eight on any old LP recording of the opera contained the magnificent final scene, from the discomfiture of Baron Ochs through the achingly beautiful final trio and the opera's quicksilver conclusion. "From track ten of CD number three" just doesn't have the same ring to it.

That poor suffering creature is right: opera is the balm that heals our souls.

A Selective Discography

The CDs listed below have been selected both for quality and availability; out-of-print LPs are also listed where appropriate.

Adams: *Nixon in China.* Original cast; Orchestra of St. Luke's conducted by Edo de Waart; Elektra/Nonesuch. A brilliant recording that captures all the score's terror and wonder.

———: *The Death of Klinghoffer.* Sylvan, Maddalena; Lyon Opera Orchestra and Chorus conducted by Kent Nagano; Elektra/Nonesuch. Better on records than in the opera house.

Bartók: *Duke Bluebeard's Castle.* Sass, Kovats; London Philharmonic conducted by Georg Solti; London. The best currently available, but try to find the old István Kertész version on LP.

Berg: *Wozzeck.* Silja, Waechter; Vienna Philharmonic conducted by Christoph von Dohnányi; London. You'll get an argument from discophiles, but the best version is still a toss-up between the old DG set led by Karl Böhm and Pierre Boulez's version on CBS.

———: *Lulu.* Stratas, Mazura; Orchestre National de France conducted by Pierre Boulez; DG. The full three-act version, in a dazzling performance by Teresa Stratas.

Bizet: *Carmen.* Price, Corelli; Vienna Philharmonic conducted by Herbert von Karajan; RCA Gold Seal. An electric recording of an electric opera. For more fun, try the old Callas recording led by Georges Prêtre on Angel.

Britten: *Death in Venice.* Pears, Shirley-Quirk; English Chamber Orchestra conducted by Steuart Bedford; London. Present at the creation, starring the tenor for whom the opera was conceived.

Glass: *Satyagraha.* Cummings, Perry; New York City Opera Orchestra and Chorus conducted by Christopher Keene; CBS. A less-than-ideal recording—terrific singing, indifferent conducting—of a magnificent work that deserves better.

Janáček: *Jenůfa.* Beňačková, others; Brno Janáček Opera Orchestra conducted by F. Jílek; Supraphon. The all-Czech cast, headed by the radiant Beňačková, makes this the one to have.

Joplin: *Treemonisha.* Soloists; Houston Grand Opera Orchestra and Chorus conducted by Gunther Schuller; DG. The only recording, and a fine one.

Mascagni: *Cavalleria rusticana.* Obraztsova, Domingo; La Scala Opera Orchestra and Chorus conducted by Georges Prêtre; Philips. And don't forget Mascagni's own recording with Gigli still available on Angel.

Leoncavallo: *Pagliacci.* Callas, Di Stefano, Gobbi; La Scala Opera Orchestra and Chorus conducted by Tullio Serafin; Angel. The Big Three, and *Cavalleria* too.

Massenet: *Werther.* De Los Angeles, Gedda; Orchestre de Paris conducted by Georges Prêtre; Angel. The ideal Werther partnered with the ideal Charlotte. But be on the lookout for Alfredo Kraus with the late Tatiana Troyanos, on an Angel recording led by Michel Plasson.

Messiaen: *Saint François d'Assise.* Soloists; Paris Opera Orchestra and Chorus conducted by Seiji Ozawa; Cybelia. Another original-cast recording, masterfully led by Ozawa.

Monteverdi: *The Coronation of Poppea.* Auger, Jones; City of London Baroque Sinfonia conducted by Richard Hickox; Virgin Classics. As per current scholarly thinking, a stripped-down version of this lush masterpiece, performed on baroque instruments.

Mozart: *The Marriage of Figaro; Così fan tutte; Don Giovanni.* Janowitz, Fischer-Dieskau; Deutsche Oper of Berlin Orchestra and Chorus conducted by Karl Böhm; DG (eight CDs). One-stop shopping, to be sure, but no one led Mozart's Italian scores with more love and insight than Böhm in these sixties' classics.

———: *The Magic Flute.* Lorengar, Prey; Vienna Philharmonic conducted by Georg Solti; London. In a crowded field, this has been the first choice for more than two decades.

Mussorgsky: *Boris Godunov.* It's out of print now, but the old Karajan recording of the Rimsky version is worth hunting down. As far as the original version is concerned, you may want to try Rostropovich's Erato recording, an uncut performance featuring his wife, the soprano Galina Vishnevskaya.

Offenbach: *The Tales of Hoffmann.* Gruberová, Domingo; Orchestre National de France conducted by Seiji Ozawa; DG. Domingo at the top of his form in one of his greatest roles.

Puccini: *La bohème.* Freni, Pavarotti; Berlin Philharmonic conducted by Herbert von Karajan; London. Far from perfect (the playing of the BPO is surprisingly sloppy), this remains the first choice for its leading man and lady.

———: *Tosca.* Price, Di Stefano, Taddei; Vienna Philharmonic conducted by Herbert von Karajan; London. A dark, brooding performance of the "shabby little shocker."

Shostakovich: *Lady Macbeth of Mtsensk.* Vishnevskaya; London Philharmonic and Ambrosian Opera Chorus conducted by Mstislav Rostropovich; DG. A fabulous, thrilling recording; it's impossible to imagine the score being played or sung any better.

Strauss: *Salome* and *Elektra.* Nilsson; Vienna Philharmonic conducted by Georg Solti; London. Definitive.

———: *Der Rosenkavalier.* Crespin, Donath; Vienna Philharmonic conducted by Georg Solti; London. One of the finest recordings, of anything, ever.

Tchaikovsky: *Eugene Onegin.* Hvorostovsky, Focile; Orchestre de Paris conducted by Semyon Bychkov; Philips. Starring the young Siberian bass matinee-idol Hvorostovsky in a role he has already made his own.

Verdi: *Otello.* Del Monaco, Tebaldi; Vienna Philharmonic conducted by Herbert von Karajan; London. Yes, Domingo is the greatest modern Otello, but Del Monaco owned the role a generation before. Here he is at his virile best.

———: *Don Carlos.* Ricciarelli, Domingo; La Scala Opera Orchestra and Chorus conducted by Claudio Abbado; DG. The five-act French version, the way it oughtta be.

Wagner: *Der Ring des Nibelungen.* Nilsson, Windgassen; Vienna Philharmonic conducted by Georg Solti; London. The first, and still the best.

———: *Tristan und Isolde.* Flagstad, Suthaus; Philharmonia Orchestra conducted by Wilhelm Furtwängler; Angel. The classic, still available and still worth hearing.

———: *Die Meistersinger.* Donath, Kollo; the Dresden State Opera Orchestra and Chorus conducted by Herbert von Karajan; Angel. Right up in there on the all-time ten-best list with Solti's *Rosenkavalier.* Hard to figure how it can be beat.

Index